T0355628

VOICES OF CAMPUS SEXUAL VIOLENCE ACTIVISTS

VOICES OF CAMPUS SEXUAL VIOLENCE ACTIVISTS

#MeToo and Beyond

ANA M. MARTÍNEZ-ALEMÁN

AND SUSAN B. MARINE

Johns Hopkins University Press

BALTIMORE

© 2023 Johns Hopkins University Press
All rights reserved. Published 2023
Printed in the United States of America on acid-free paper
9 8 7 6 5 4 3 2 1

Johns Hopkins University Press
2715 North Charles Street
Baltimore, Maryland 21218
www.press.jhu.edu

Library of Congress Cataloging-in-Publication Data is available.

A catalog record for this book is available from the British Library.

ISBN 978-1-4214-4770-4 (hardcover)
ISBN 978-1-4214-4771-1 (ebook)

Special discounts are available for bulk purchases of this book. For more information, please contact Special Sales at specialsales@jh.edu.

To all the

campus sexual violence activists

who shared their stories with us,

and to those activists

who continue to remind

our institutions that

ending sexual violence

is their responsibility

♥

CONTENTS

PREFACE

We began this project in the months before the COVID-19 pandemic changed all our lives. In the spring of 2020, many colleges and universities attended by campus sexual violence activists shut down all in-person campus life and sent students home to finish their courses remotely. When we were able to begin our conversations with campus sexual violence activists in the early summer of 2020, most had been living on or near their campuses and planned to return to their campuses the following fall. We all anticipated that, by the coming autumn, colleges and universities would reopen and that our student activists would return to campus to continue their sexual violence activism. But by the late summer of 2020, it was clear that the 2020–2021 academic year would be dramatically altered by COVID, as colleges and universities across the country turned to online-only instruction or to severely restricted on-campus life. Unable to meet with us in person during the pandemic, our campus sexual violence activists shared with us their experiences through videoconferencing.

As researchers, our motivation to give voice to campus sexual violence activists is a product of our scholarship on gender in higher education, certainly. As scholars, we've dedicated much of our work to examine how gender is the discursive currency in colleges and universities and how gender informs institutional structures that limit gender freedoms. As former practitioners, we look to research to provide institutions with change propositions, for tangible ways to create and support gender equity. But a deeper and more fierce impulse gave rise to this project. Students who dedicate their college years to ending sexual violence on campus shoulder a burden that is not theirs to carry, and they are often silenced and dismissed. The work of changing campus cultures that foment, provoke, and sustain sexual violence belongs to administrative leaders imbued with institutional power, not students. Campus sexual violence activists know this. Activists' experiences reveal that they recognize that their impotence is the product of institutional disavowal of responsibility. As scholars, we hypothesized this, and the campus sexual violence activists who shared their experiences with us corroborated our supposition. We wanted to give voice to the activists themselves.

We wish to thank the graduate students at Boston College's Lynch School of Education and Human Development who assisted with this project. Each brought a sensibility to the project that enabled us to work through the constraints brought by COVID-19, and each contributed analytical acumen that enriched the project at every turn. We are especially indebted to

Allison Yarri, Sara Sparks, and Marisa Lally; to each of them we offer our heartfelt thanks. Along the way, other graduate students have pitched in to move the project along, including Asuka Harimoto, and our thanks go out to them as well. Most of all, we are profoundly grateful to campus sexual violence activists for being who they are, for what they do, and for their tenacity and doggedness in the face of intractable campus cultures.

Note to the Reader

Campus sexual violence activism is always ever-changing and responsive to historic and current sociopolitical and cultural forces. This book is a snapshot in time of campus sexual violence activism by student activists in 2020–2021.

VOICES OF CAMPUS SEXUAL VIOLENCE ACTIVISTS

INTRODUCTION

In June 2019 the *New York Times* reported that a "new wave of campus activism" had organized on college and university campuses to combat the culture of sexual violence. Energized by #MeToo and the Harvey Weinstein trial, the college student activists profiled by the *New York Times* spoke not only of organizing across institutions through social media but also in the tradition of the on-the-ground college activism of the 1960s (Hartocollis 2019).

Who are these college students engaged in sexual violence activism on college campuses today? What are the strategies and tools they use to enact change in the #MeToo era? How do Gen Z activists use collective mobilization and activism through social media as well as long-established campus organizing in the service of eradicating sexual violence on campus? How do sexual violence activists engage with their institutions? Today, student activists speak passionately about their rights, their expectations for how they will be treated by college officials, and their institution's responsibility to provide preventative education and compassionate advocacy.

The Obama-era "Dear Colleague" Letters (Ali 2011) were designed to further clarify the roles and responsibilities of educational institution officials responding to sexual harassment. They announced a new emphasis on sexual harassment and sexual violence on the basis of assigned sex, gender identity, and transgender status. Reflecting the reconceptualization of gender, gender identity, and gender-based violence, and consistent with college student sexual violence activists' generational awareness, the spirit of the "Dear Colleague" Letter energized and empowered campus activists. The ascendance of the Trump administration in 2016, however, rendered those changes a relic of the distant past. The appointment of Betsy DeVos as the United States Secretary of Education by President Donald J. Trump in 2017 signaled a sea change in sexual harassment and sexual violence policies and practices that would shift campus activism back to its pre-Obama objectives.

In May 2020 US Secretary of Education Betsy DeVos announced the Final Rule under Title IX of the Education Amendments of 1972, specifying a set of modifications for institutional processes for adjudicating sexual harassment and violence. Specifically, this Trump-era ruling on Title IX narrowed the definition of sexual harassment and heightened evidentiary standards that activists and scholars believe will deter victims from reporting, effectively returning us to a time when "rape and harassment in schools were ignored and swept under the rug" according to the President of the National Women's Law Center. Under the Title IX revisions, cross-examination of accusers and the accused must be conducted in live hearings in which institutional Title IX officers and investigators are not present. Colleges and universities can no longer hear cases of sexual violence committed off campus in fraternity parties or unaffiliated off-campus houses. Additionally, these revisions to Title IX sexual harassment and violence processes could be interpreted by college and university officials as an encouragement to choose more informal processes in order to avoid the costlier prescribed processes (Gersen 2020).

Many of these regulatory changes to Title IX have been challenged by such groups as the American Civil Liberties Union, and currently 17 states have filed a Complaint for Declaratory and Injunctive Relief to prevent the implementation of these revisions to Title IX (ACLU 2020). Alleging that the revisions will effectively offer students less protection from sexual harassment and that the new investigative and adjudicative rules will discourage complaints and apply uniform procedures to all types of complaints, the complaint sought to make these regulatory revisions unlawful.

In sum, the DeVos era Title IX regulations sought to alter campus policies and practices related to sexual violence prevention, reporting, and prosecution, and they undoubtedly energized student sexual violence activism. Throughout our book and in the conceptual framing of the research that informs it, we used Basile and Saltzman's (2002, 9–10) definition of sexual violence and assault as any nonconsensual sexual act (whether actualized or interrupted); nonconsensual sexual acts such as verbal and/or behavioral sexual taunting are framed as sexual harassment. Certainly, these are associated, interlocking, and often analogous terms, but as we heard activists' stories, it was clear that these (somewhat fluid) distinctions were made.

In the pages that follow, we center the voices and experiences of college students engaged in sexual violence activism. High-profile college activists discussed the ways in which they identified, selected, and understood their strategies for effective sexual violence activism in the era of social media and Trump politics. Many were enrolled in colleges and universities when they spoke with us and have since graduated, while others were recent graduates. Through interviews with current and former campus activists, we captured the strategies and tools they use to enact change on college campuses today. We mapped the terrain of the work of a specific, active, and visible population of student activists, whose work to influence institutional, state, and federal policy stands as a testament to the rich legacies of 1960s activism and signals a new wave of social media–centered work in this new era.

Among recent generations of students, social media are used as an effective communications tool to mobilize campus collective action and to gain wider acceptance of their causes (Morgan and Davis 2019). Social media also brings sociopolitical causes to campuses. Digital activism outside of the campus grounds is adopted by college students today much like they have adopted causes external to the campus for much of higher education's history in the United States (Thelin 2018, 7).

But social media activism against sexual harassment and sexual violence, such as the activism subsumed under the hashtags #MeToo and #TimesUp, has inspired and emboldened campus activists in ways unavailable to previous generations. For example, a spate of campus sexual violence protests at the University of Nebraska and the University of Massachusetts in the fall of 2021 garnered media attention on a national scale (Hartocollis and Heyward 2021). Commenting on this trend, a faculty member at Miami University said that "students are using social media to document their colleges' betrayal of the promises they made to keep students safe." The documentation creates a 'digital archive' of the unmet demands, mishandled complaints, and concerning statistics—not only at one's own college, but at hundreds of others" (Bellows, 2021).

Student activism has recently resurged, and evidence suggests that participation in it has a meaningful and lasting effect for students and institutions alike (Morgan and Davis 2019, xvii). A goal in writing this book was to examine the recent reigniting of student activism in influencing policy and practice. To that end, we asked student activists to reflect on four aspects of their work: (1) what strategies campus sexual violence activists engage in today; (2) how they mobilized and drafted other students; (3) how they employed social media and digital activism to further their causes; and (4) how student activists mediate campus policies with their institutional leaders.

Though traditional news media have covered high-profile cases of campus sexual violence complaints, such as Andrea Pino's and Annie Clark's against the University of North Carolina in 2013 and many others before it (Pérez-Peña 2014), the landscape of sexual violence activism on college campuses was ignited in 2017 by the power of social media, in particular by Twitter. Though established by activist Tarana Burke in 2006, the "MeToo" movement was reignited on Twitter with #MeToo, raising the consciousness of new digital generations (Li et al. 2021; Deal et al. 2020).

STUDENT SEXUAL VIOLENCE ACTIVISTS

In January and February 2020 we initiated the search to identify student sexual violence activists on US campuses. We sought to identify campus sexual violence activists (CSVAs) (borrowing the abbreviation first used by Harris and Linder 2017) who were currently enrolled in US institutions or who were alumni of the class of 2014 or later. These were students who were active after the 2011 "Dear Colleague" Letter and during the #MeToo movement. We developed the activist list by recruiting student and alumni activists who had been publicly named in reputable news sources such as the *New York Times*, the *Washington Post*, and the *Chronicle of Higher Education*. Student activists were also identified in searches of college or university newspapers or named in the documentary *The Hunting Ground* (Dick and Ziering 2015). Online searches using search engine keywords also led us to student activists featured in other periodicals, sometimes confirming those we had previously identified.

Throughout the winter months of 2020, we scoured these sources, contacted key informants in institutions for referrals, and eventually settled on a list of publicly named individuals of all genders. Once participants were contacted to consent to an interview, we asked for referrals to other student activists. We made extensive effort to identify racially and ethnically diverse student activists in both private and public colleges and universities with varying student body size, and campus location (e.g., urban versus rural) across the United States. We did not recruit any student activists from our own institutions.

To listen to and to center the voices of student sexual violence activists, we conducted individual interviews with student sexual violence. More detailed information regarding our procedure is available in the Methodological Appendix. After receiving approval to use human subjects from our respective institutional review boards, we contacted 36 student activists to consent to and participate in an interview. When invited to participate, none challenged the "activist" characterization of their work nor did any correct the characterization of their work. We recorded and transcribed the interview with participant consent and with their understanding that they could choose to remain anonymous. Only one of the activists interviewed chose anonymity, but at times a few did request that certain information remain "off the record." In all, 22 student sexual violence activists from 14 different institutions consented to be interviewed and to contribute their voices to this book. Participating activists graduated from or were enrolled in institutions that vary in type, mission, and setting: small and large private, large and small public, historically Black college and university, small liberal arts college (secular and religiously affiliated), urban, suburban, rural, East Coast, Mid-Atlantic, Rockies, and West Coast.

It was our intention to interview student activists in person where possible, but we were thwarted by the onset of the COVID-19 pandemic in March 2020. Many of the activists had to leave their campuses and return home during this time, and their course and work schedules were suddenly uncertain for a period of time—and sometimes unresolved for the remainder of the spring semester into the early summer. By April 2020 it became clear that in-person interviewing could not be conducted given COVID-19 restrictions and safety. After these student activists were settled and able to manage their daily agenda, we were able to schedule interviews on a video communications platform (Zoom). Though delayed and stymied by the COVID-19 pandemic, we interviewed students on Zoom in the early summer and into the early fall of 2020.

Our conversations with students were designed to listen to their perspectives on the what, the how, and the why of their campus sexual violence activism. We asked them to share with us the strategies in which they engaged: how they mobilized and drafted other students to sexual violence activism. We asked about their motivation for sexual violence activism and why sexual violence activism was a personal commitment. We asked activists to share the goals of their activism, both immediate and long term, and the ways their activism affected their sense of self, their health, and mental well-being. We prompted them to talk about the activism strategies they employed on campus and their methods to mediate campus policies and interact with their institution's administrators and faculty. We probed the impact and effect of the #MeToo movement on their activism and their use of social media in their activism. Student activists often shared views on their institutions' responses to sexual violence that were framed by their own perceptions of dominant discourses that inform campus culture at their college or university. We asked activists to recommend ways administrators could build stronger partnerships with student activists to enact positive change. And though not part of our initial plan, we asked activists to comment on the effects of the COVID-19 pandemic on their activism.

The interviews generated rich and robust empirical data that were managed through typical qualitative social science research methods. Using qualitative software data, we used emergent coding to determine what was significant in the interview data (Saldaña 2015). Separately, we continued with thematic coding and constant comparative coding until we determined analytic groupings (Rallis and Rossman 2012). Additionally, two graduate student members of our research team coded each interview transcript as well to compare coded data for reliability and trustworthiness. After coding was compared across all four members of the research team, we assessed data patterns and grouped the data into thematic categories (Charmaz 2006). Finally, the research team discussed the thematic categories or themes and reconciled some incongruences across the researchers to ensure that our interpretations of student activists' voices were reasonable and well founded.

These interview data are the personal perceptions, emotions, impressions, and states of mind of campus sexual violence activists that are not often attended to and that are not commonly and customarily honored. Historically, as researchers, we have rightly focused attention on the *survivors* of campus sexual violence, but rarely have we given attention to those campus activists who dedicate themselves to preventing and ending sexual violence on college and university campuses. This book is an opportunity for them to be heard.

In this book, we foreground the voices of campus sexual violence activists across a range of identities and institutional settings. Here are brief introductions to the CSVAs who so generously shared their experiences with us. We have respected how they wished to be identified (race/ethnicity, gender pronouns, first name only). Because we often refer to the activists by their chosen first names throughout the book, their profiles are in alphabetical order by first name.

Alexia Petasis (she/her) is a graduate of the University of Maryland, Baltimore County. She identifies as a white female who is tricultural and trilingual, in addition to being a first-generation American. While at UMBC, Alexia pursued an individualized plan of study, which allowed her to combine her skills in choreography with social justice work. As a capstone project, Alexia chose to do a dance that brought to light "the experiences of survivors of domestic sex trafficking from the point of view of the victim" (McCaffrey 2019). This project drew attention to the manipulation and exploitation that survivors can face in human trafficking. Currently, Alexia is a childcare worker. When the pandemic ends, she hopes to find ways to actively engage in activism again within her community.

Andrea Pino-Silva (she/her) is a graduate of the University of North Carolina at Chapel Hill, where she studied political science. Andrea identifies as a first-generation college student, queer Latina/Cuban American, cisgender woman, who is the daughter of Cuban immigrants. Since graduating, Andrea has been a part of grassroots organizing and radical storytelling, co-authored *We Believe You: Survivors of Campus Sexual Assault Speak Out* (2016) and cofounded a national survivor advocacy organization, End Rape on Campus, in 2013. She has spoken at various universities and supported students in learning their rights under Title IX, as well as changing their campus sexual assault policies. Her advocacy work has been featured in popular media sources like the *New York Times*, *Good Morning America*, *Vogue*, CNN, and more. Andrea was also one of the main interviewees in *The Hunting Ground*, a documentary about exposing rape on US college campuses. Currently, she works as a communications consultant and is a PhD student.

Anika (she/her) is a 2019 graduate of the University of California at Irvine, where she studied public health policy and English. Anika identifies as Bangladeshi Muslim and as a cisgender woman. She is also a first-generation student from a low-income background. She was hailed for her activism by the UCI Center for Student Leadership. She was a student leader within an organization known as HEART Women & Girls, a national organization working to end all forms of gendered harassment and violence for Muslims as well as provide resources to improve sexual health. Anika's activism also included building bridges to Muslim communities on campus and working to improve services for students of color at the campus sexual assault advocacy center. Her work also centered the experiences of Muslim women and intersected with efforts to oppose sweatshops and counter post-9/11 Islamophobia. She now works as an administrative specialist for another university.

Anja Chivukula (she/her) is a graduate of Barnard College. She identifies as a mixed-race Indian and Ashkenazi Jewish woman. At Barnard, she was a member of No Red Tape, a Columbia-Barnard activist group centered around ending sexual and domestic violence on campuses through pushing for direct policy changes, creating education programs to prevent violence and combat rape culture, and providing direct support to survivors. In her time with No Red Tape, Anja fought for improved access to health care for students, improved Title IX policies to protect and support survivors, organized a panel following the Brett Kavanaugh hearings, wrote op-eds and petitions to garner the attention of the administration, and participated in a four-day sit-in in a student building. She is pursuing a graduate degree.

Coral Barrera (she/her) was a University of California Irvine peer educator at the time of the interview and worked at a rape crisis center. Coral supervised a 24-hour sexual assault hotline and was in the process of applying to law schools and/or master's programs in public policy and public health.

Danu Mudannayke (she/her) is a 2020 graduate of Harvard College, Cambridge, Massachusetts, where she majored in visual and environmental studies. During her time in college, Danu was a very involved member of the sexual violence activist group Harvard Can Do Better. Originally from England, Danu is a first-generation Black student who took an active role with her peers to challenge sexual assault and violence policies at Harvard. Among other actions taken, Danu authored an op-ed in the student newspaper (the *Harvard Crimson*) advocating for the termination of the faculty dean (Ronald Sullivan) affiliated with Winthrop, her residential house. According to Danu, Sullivan, a member of Harvey Weinstein's defense team, was dismissive of Winthrop students' concerns and was perceived by students as inflexible and unwilling to listen to students' concerns. Danu currently lives and works in England and is planning to pursue a career in the film industry.

Eli Dunn (they/them) is a graduate of Middlebury College. Eli identifies as Black, nonbinary, and queer and is a part of the working class. Currently, they work as a union organizer and a canvasser at the Brooklyn Movement Center. While a student at Middlebury College, Eli faced college discipline after posting a list of male students accused of sexual misconduct. When asked if they thought their actions would impact future opportunities, they said stood by their decision, saying, "This harm is being done by specific people and by specific individuals, and if we want to move toward a conversation about healing, accountability, and growth, there needs to be some acknowledgment that harm was done" (Walsh 2018).

Emily Arpino (she/her) is a graduate of the State University of New York at Geneseo. She identifies as a white cisgender woman as well as queer and neurodivergent. At Geneseo, Emily was involved with the Women's Action Coalition, a group dedicated to educating the campus community about women's issues, including sexual assault and harassment. With this group, she organized the annual Take Back the Night March. Emily currently works as a community sex educator at Planned Parenthood.

Julia Paris (she/her) is a graduate of Stanford University and at the time of our interview was pursuing a master's degree in public policy at Stanford. At Stanford, she worked on a committee to provide recommendations for the new Title IX policy when the DeVos regulations were released. She is also a founding member of SVFree Stanford, a sexual violence activism group formed during the COVID-19 pandemic.

Kara Burke (she/her) was a senior at the State University of New York at Geneseo at the time of our interview. She identifies as a white woman. Kara interviewed survivors of sexual assault for an exposé on a fraternity for the school newspaper. Following her piece, an anonymous Instagram account, @Shareyourstorygeneseo, was created to share stories of sexual assault and harassment at Geneseo. Reading these stories prompted Kara to organize a "Take Back Geneseo" march during move-in weekend to protest administration inaction and bring awareness. Kara also works with the InterGreek Council to address sexual assault and violence against women in Geneseo Greek Life. After graduation, she plans to pursue a career in journalism.

Kayla Edwards-Friedland (they/she) was a junior at time of interview at Georgetown University. They identify as a Black and white bisexual woman. They are a first-generation student from a low-income background. Kayla is a member of the Black Survivors Coalition at Georgetown and participated in a weeklong sit-in in the president's office after a list of demands went unacknowledged. The list of demands included hiring Black counseling clinicians and Black trauma specialists as well as extending the hours of health services. They plan to continue organizing post-graduation.

Logan Deutchman (she/her) is a 2021 graduate of Westminster College in Salt Lake City, Utah. Logan is the founder of a campus group on women's empowerment and was active in working with Professor Nicole Bedera on conducting research on survivor experiences at Westminster. Logan advocated for provision of a 40-hour training on sexual violence trauma for student leaders, faculty, and staff at Westminster.

Lynnea Doshi (she/her) was a current pre-med student at University of California Los Angeles at the time of our interview, who was planning to graduate in 2022. She identifies as Asian (Indian) and female and was a student activist. She was enrolled in the UCLA Honors program. Lynnea has worked as a CARE (Campus Assault Resources and Education) peer educator since 2019.

Maya (she/her) is a 2020 graduate of Georgetown University who identifies as a Black cisgender woman. Maya majored in government and held minors in religion, ethics, and world affairs and creative writing and studied abroad in Israel as a junior. She was a founding member of the Black Survivors Coalition (BSC), an activist group that formed in 2019 as a subset of the original activist group (The STOP Coalition). Administrator inaction after many years of activism by student groups led the BSC to occupy Healy Hall (an administrative building) in February 2020 for 76 hours. During this occupation, the BSC advanced a list of demands related to improving services for survivors and addressing lapses in the adjudication process. Maya is currently a graduate student at the Harvard Divinity School and continues her work in community organizing, writing, and activism.

Michelle Dickey (she/her) is a 2020 *summa cum laude* graduate of University of California Los Angeles, where she studied human biology and society. Michelle was an active member of the Campus Assault Resource and Education peer educator corps, a group of students dedicated to violence prevention and awareness among her peers. Michelle has been involved in sexual assault activism since high school, when she was involved in a group of students working at Casa de las Madres in San Francisco. During her time at UCLA, she conducted workshops to provide her peers with information about safety, consent, and culture change. She now works as a customer care and quality assurance specialist at a health care agency in California.

Morgan Mullings (they/them) is a 2019 graduate of the University of Maryland, Baltimore County, where they majored in media and communication studies with minors in English and cinematic arts. They identify as Black, Liberian, Jamaican, nonbinary, fat, and queer. Morgan was an intern at the women's center during their time at UMBC and was actively involved in activism efforts to end sexual violence at the university, participating in open forums (including audiences with the university's president) and Take Back the Night. Morgan is currently working as a patient care coordinator in Baltimore and writing poetry. In the future, they hope to facilitate a writing workshop to facilitate healing for Black people who are survivors of sexual assault and intimate partner violence.

Nadia BenAissa (she/her) is a graduate of University of Maryland, Baltimore County. She identifies as a mixed race, Arab-American cisgender woman, as well as queer and Muslim. Nadia created the group We Believe You, a sexual assault activism group that centered survivor support. When UMBC faced lawsuits for the mishandling of Title IX cases, We Believe You was called to action to participate in campus-wide protests and advocate for survivors in conversations with university administration. UMBC created the Retriever Courage initiative in response to the lawsuit and student protests. Part of this initiative included making changes to the Title IX office, a process that Nadia was thoroughly involved in. Nadia was an original member of the Inclusion Council that advises the Office of Equity and Inclusion, and she continues to serve on this council post-graduation.

Nylah Burton (she/her) is a graduate of Howard University. She identifies as a Black cisgender woman with bipolar disorder.

After graduating from Howard, Nylah created the Black Survivors Healing Fund, a fundraising effort to support the financial needs of sexual assault survivors from Howard University. She highlights the importance of monetary support in healing. Nylah emphasizes the importance of these funds being unrestricted because survivors have different immediate needs that include rent, food, therapy, clothing, self-care, or simply things that make them happy. Nylah currently works as a freelance writer; her work has appeared in *Bustle, New York Magazine, Essence, Vogue,* and the *Huffington Post,* to name a few. She is working on a memoir to be released by Penguin Books.

Rebecca Sobel (she/her) graduated in 2020 from Princeton University, where she studied economics and environmental studies. Identifying as white and Jewish, Rebecca became involved in activism in her junior year to change Princeton's reporting and adjudication policies. Along with other activists, Rebecca planned and executed a student-led protest outside of the administration building in May of 2019 that lasted for eight days. The activists involved in the sit-in issued a list of eleven specific demands, including additional transparency about the reporting system, punishments for those found responsible for assault, and calling for the dismissal of the Title IX Coordinator. The sit-in lasted several days and followed months of other forms of protest related to these issues. Rebecca now works in management consulting.

Sophia Kim (she/her) was a student at Boston University at the time of the interview double majoring in psychology and English. She identifies as an Asian American, cisgender woman. She is a first-generation student from a low-income background. Sophia is an administrator for the Instagram account Campus Survivors, which posts anonymous accounts of sexual assault on college campuses, primarily in the greater Boston area, and provides resources for survivors. The goal of the account is to provide a space for survivors to share their stories and receive support. The account has caught the attention of university administrators, and the group hopes to use that attention to create change.

Subhadra (she/her) graduated from Stanford University in 2021 with a degree in computer science and a minor in gender and sexuality studies. She identifies as a South Asian woman and a first-generation immigrant. Subhadra pursued activism at Stanford aimed to enact policy change.

Yashica Kataria (she/her) is a political science major at Boston University. Yashica identifies as an Indian (South Asian), female, a first-generation college student, and immigrant. During COVID-19, she has helped organize socially distant protests involving over 600 students at Boston University, along with her co-founders at Campus Survivors. Campus Survivors is a program that allows survivors of sexual assault to share their stories anonymously. In addition, Campus Survivors is able to advocate for and support survivors through fundraising, social media engagement, emails sent to administration, and more. Their work has been highlighted in the *Boston Globe, BU Today, Daily Free Press*, and the "Beauty, Brains, and Baggage" podcast.

AUTHOR POSITIONALITY

Ana M. Martínez-Alemán (she/her) is a professor of higher education at the Lynch School of Education and Human Development at Boston College, where she serves as associate dean of Faculty and Academics. A white, bilingual Cuban immigrant woman, she has been an administrator and a faculty member in both public and private tertiary institutions. As a scholar and researcher, Martínez-Alemán turns her attention to gender and race/ethnicity in higher education.

Susan B. Marine (she/her) is a professor of higher education, where she serves as Vice Provost of Advances in Learning
and Teaching at Merrimack College. A white lesbian cis woman,
Marine has spent most of the last three decades as a researcher,
activist, prevention educator, and professional survivor advocate
on four different US college campuses. She was the founding
director of the Harvard University Office of Sexual Assault
Prevention and Response and serves on the national board of
the Take Back the Night Foundation. Marine also serves as a
consultant to numerous institutions and community agencies
on preventing and responding to sexual violence in higher education. Her areas of scholarly focus are student and faculty
activist identity development, and LGBTQIA survivor healing, agency, and thriving.

ORGANIZATION OF THE BOOK

The book's opening chapter charts the historical context and
foundation for the emergence of sexual violence activism on college and university campuses in the United States. Chapter 1
traces the history of the movement to end sexual violence on
campus back to its origins in the Civil Rights movement through
today's racial and social justice activism. The coalitions formed
to oppose violence, their political commitments, and the legal
and public policy work they quietly forged through collaboration
with key figures in the federal government are examined. The
modern-day origins of the campus rape movement and federal
responses to it, stretching back to the 1980s and the advent of
the Violence Against Women Act, is also explored.

The advent of #MeToo, the role of technology in raising the
visibility of the problem, and the neoliberal practice of "one size
fits all" approaches to rape prevention is examined and prob-
lematized in the book's second chapter. In chapter 2, pivotal mo-

ments in campus rape activism and its impact, specifically over the last decade, round out the book's historical overview. This chapter sets the scene to better understand what motivates current campus sexual violence activists, the investments they make in activism, the effects of their activism on their identities as activists, and their perceptions of various institutional relationships that either promote or hinder their antiviolence advocacy on campus.

The succeeding chapters in which we hear the voices of campus sexual violence activists are the heart of the book. In these chapters, we meet 22 campus sexual violence activists who shared their reflections on the motivation for their activism, their perceptions of the impact of their activism on their identities, and their assessments of their respective institution's responses to their activism. Chapters 3 and 4 are dedicated to the four unifying themes we heard throughout our interviews with campus activists. In chapter 3, the students talk about what motivates them to engage in campus sexual violence activism and their understanding of their identities as campus sexual violence activists. In chapter 4, the student activists talk about the strategies and approaches to campus sexual violence activism on their campuses, whether successful or failed. The risks and rewards of campus sexual violence activism for activists and the impact of institutional practices and policies on activists are also discussed. In this chapter, activists catalog the personal highs and lows of their activism, the emotional and physical toll of their activism, and its impact on their campus relationships, academic progress, and future careers.

In the concluding chapters, we synthesize the voices of student activists and present conclusions to inform campus policies and practices. We discuss how students' accounts of campus sexual violence activism can provide campus leaders with heightened awareness of the motivations and justifications for the antiviolence work that inspires and animates student activists on campus. We take up sexual violence activism as a form of student engagement whose developmental effects are rarely considered, but must be.

Based on the data gathered from student activists, chapter 5 presents recommendations for institutional responses to sexual violence activism. We contend that institutional decision-making must consider the experiences of student activists working on the front lines for change on their campuses, along with other considerations such as compliance with Title IX and calls for due process in adjudication. Therefore, we present institutional leaders with recommended action to effectively use activist–student affairs staff alliances to enable meaningful change on campuses. In the book's sixth and concluding chapter, we consider the need for institutional change. Here, we put forth a call for a "cultural reset" in institutional culture and power necessary for sexual violence to end on college campuses.

Chapter 1

LOOKING BACK TO LOOK FORWARD

Highly visible social movements and the urgency of those who propel them have a way of seeming new even when they are embedded in decades of struggle. To wit: the movement to end campus sexual violence originated in the early twentieth century, fomented and sustained by strands of the civil rights movement of the 1950s, the women's movements of the 1970s, and the emergence of intersectional feminism in the 1990s (Driessen 2020). The #MeToo movement, while not singularly focused on campus sexual violence, amplified attention to the problem (Pettit 2020). #MeToo's ubiquity on social and mainstream media, and the wave after wave of survivors surfacing and claiming its mantle, revealed the vast grip sexual violence has on American society.

To understand the waves of activism and how they have contributed to the formulation of contemporary activism against sexual violence, it is important to revisit the path leading to the emergence of both the hashtag and the groundswell. The lessons of each successive wave of sexual violence activism help to make sense of what contemporary activists know and understand as well as what they tend to forget.

CONSCIOUSNESS AWAKENS

The 1970s are often referenced as the founding era of the rape crisis movement (Brownmiller 1975). In decades prior, however, activists were banding together to name and oppose rape and to insist on accountability for the crime, even at great personal peril. Many Black women survived (or didn't survive) rape during slavery and reconstruction. The dehumanization of Black people, women especially, created the conditions leading to rampant sexual victimization, typically with impunity for those who perpetrated it. Not surprisingly, then, the earliest documentation of antirape activism emanates from Black community organizing.

More than a century before the advent of the first rape crisis center, Black women were naming sexual violence as a tool of racist oppression and organizing to confront and end it (McGuire 2004, 911; White 2001, 14). Indeed, rape has always been used as a tool of domination. Its disparate imprint on the lives of Women of Color since the earliest days of white colonizers engaging in chattel enslavement of Black and Indigenous people, rape has been a means to control Women of Color (Freedman 2013, 21; Harris 2020, 2; Linder 2018, 9). Post–Civil War reconstruction brought little relief: Frances Thompson, a Black woman living in Memphis, testified to a congressional committee in 1867 about being held at gunpoint and raped in her home by seven white men during the Memphis race riot

(McGuire 2004, 908–909). During this time period, there was no reward for speaking out about one's victimization. Survivors would have been motivated only by their own conviction in their right to have a voice and to use it. Scholars have argued persuasively that this is the throughline that connects the decision to speak up about one's experience with sexual assault to refusal of racist subjugation in other domains (McGuire 2004, 2010). Women of Color, accustomed to but steadfastly resistant to this subjugation, led the charge to oppose rape alongside other forms of racial discrimination.

In the years leading up to the civil rights movement, one notable case of organized resistance was initiated on behalf of survivor Recy Taylor. In 1944 Taylor was kidnapped and raped by six white men in rural Alabama as she was walking home from church. Trading on the stereotype of the Jezebel (West 1995, 462), Taylor's attackers depicted her as a "prostitute" and justified their aggression as their response to a seductress. Taylor spoke out about the rape and sought justice from the local police (Buirski 2017). Taylor's case was unusual, not only because she demanded accountability but because media coverage of the case sparked an activist uprising. Led by the NAACP (National Association for the Advancement of Colored People) and Rosa Parks, the leaders of this uprising organized campaigns to pressure the local prosecutor to arrest and try the accused. Even so, and despite confessions to the crime by several of the men, no charges were filed, and no convictions were ever obtained (McGuire 2010, 8–9).

Parks visited Abbeville, Alabama after the incident to interview Recy Taylor and was chased off the premises by the local sheriff. Undaunted, she and others from the Montgomery chapter of the NAACP organized the Alabama Committee for

Equal Justice for Mrs. Recy Taylor, headquartered in Harlem in
New York City (McGuire 2010, 15). In addition to many un-
named foot soldiers, Black luminaries including W. E. B. Du
Bois, Mary Church Terrell, Countee Culleen, and Langston
Hughes advocated vocally for Taylor's case (Chan 2017). An extensive campaign to obtain the support of Governor Chauncey
Sparks—a future acolyte of George Wallace, who would later
become governor himself—resulted in tepid compliance and
investigation of the local sheriff. Several of the men implicated
acknowledged that they had sex with Taylor but argued it had
been consensual and involved payment. One participant in the
assault admitted that Taylor was crying and begging to go home,
but not a single one of the accused was indicted. The case, and
the activism surrounding it, eventually withered away. In 2011 the
Alabama legislature issued an official apology to Taylor, by then
age 91 (Chan 2017).

The NAACP activism represented a significant shift in strategy. Prior to the campaign for Taylor, Black women experiencing rape in the United States would be either required to speak
up as individuals or shamed into silence; they were rarely able
to pursue criminal charges. Cases of white women accusing
Black men or boys of rape, or even of casual physical contact or
gestures, ended in lynching, as in the case of the murder of Emmett Till (Crowe 2018). The Committee for Equal Justice represented the first movement seeking redress for the dual crimes
of rape and racism, which were fully permitted by the white su-
premacist criminal justice system in Alabama.

Five years later, a similar coalition formed to advocate for
justice for another Black survivor, Gertrude Perkins. Known as
the Citizens Committee to Aid Perkins, this group unsuccess-
fully advocated for an indictment of her attacker. Perkins's plight
was connected to the larger push for Black civil rights in Ala-

bama; journalists of the era noted her self-advocacy "had as much to do with the Montgomery bus boycott and its creation as anyone on earth" (McGuire 2004, 912). Sadly, the Taylor case was only one of many examples: the histories of Black women, both leaders and everyday citizens, are replete with stories of rape wielded as a tool of racist subjugation against foremothers and contemporaries alike (Hobson and DeYoung 2021). While Black men often remained silent about this violence, Black women spoke out, risking their "respectability" as well as their lives.

These and other examples of activism by Black women at midcentury long preceded the second wave of the women's movement and represented principled, sophisticated, and well-coordinated resistance to the tolerance of sexual violence. This explains why, when telling the story of resistance to rape, we must keep the impassioned, strategic, and multilevel approaches of these activists at the forefront. Parks's, and other activists' commitment to building a diverse and inclusive movement are present in the work and in political commitments of the campus sexual violence activists discussed in this book. These campus activists make clear that the meetings and marches they lead are inspired and informed by earlier activists' commitment to inclusive activism.

THE FIRST RAPE CRISIS CENTERS

The 1970s and the burgeoning of the second wave of feminism brought shifts in consciousness along many different aspects of women's lived experience, and in particular, experiences with sexual and domestic violence. Consciousness-raising groups became the site of women's testimony to surviving sexual violence; these were also the places where women came to terms with the frightening normalcy of rape (Rose 1977, 76). Women began to mobilize to oppose sexual violence, as theorizing about its origins and impact proliferated. In her landmark 1975 book, *Against Our Will: Men, Women, and Rape,* Susan Brownmiller gave voice to the idea that rape represented more than an individual act of violation, instead calling it foundational to men's subjugation of women in a sexist society. The scourge of sexual violence against trans women also garnered newfound attention in this era. In the years after the Stonewall riots—the uprisings against police brutality at a bar in New York City's Greenwich Village—Sylvia Rivera implored the burgeoning gay rights movement to recognize the rampant rape and other forms of abuse she and other trans people survived in the prison system (Patterson 2016, xii).

In large cities and rural towns alike, women began to create rape crisis centers (often just a room, a phone, and a bed) for survivors. In 1971 San Francisco Women Against Rape and the DC Rape Crisis Center were both established (Driessen 2020, 566). By 1979 one thousand rape crisis centers existed across the country (Collins and Whalen 1989, 61). These centers proliferated on college campuses, often connected to or embedded in the local community center (Jessup-Anger, Lopez, and Koss 2018, 10). Women of Color led the charge against sexual violence, naming sexual violence as both a raced and gendered phenomenon. For example, the Combahee River Collective (2014, 271–280) spoke out against the sexism Black women faced in the pressure to remain silent about violence by Black men, as well as the racism they faced in social movement work dominated by white women (Scott 2000, 797). The same year the Combahee River Collective published its manifesto, activists opposing the objectifying effects of pornography organized the first Take Back the Night March in the United States, which was held in 1978 in San Francisco (Greensite 2003).

Led by feminists and their allies, community-centered rape crisis movements brought significant attention to the problem of rape and sexual harassment, advocating both for additional resources for survivors and for widespread legal and policy change. Yet with few exceptions, activism opposing rape on college campuses was not visible or documented until the 1980s. Research on the prevalence of sexual violence on college campuses dates back to the late 1950s, when Clifford Kirkpatrick and Eugene Kanin published two studies on men's aggression against women on campus (Klein 2018, 66). Kirkpatrick and Kanin found nearly 56% of women surveyed "reported themselves offended by male students at least once during the academic year" (Kirkpatrick and Kanin 1957, 53). Despite this alarming percentage, few studies aimed to replicate their work.

Journalistic and first-person accounts of collegiate women surviving rape began to surface in the 1980s (Johnston 2011; Koss and Rutherford 2018), though little was documented about the factors that engendered the occurrence of rape on college campuses and its ubiquity. Student activists were beginning to mobilize and amplify the issue's urgency in pockets of activity around the country. Radcliffe College students organized its first Take Back the Night March in 1980 (Harrington 2017), and hundreds of students at Barnard College gathered in 1988 to hold that institution's first march (Take Back the Night Foundation 2021).

Localized awareness became national headlines when Mary Koss and colleagues published a landmark study documenting the fact that 26% of college women experienced rape or other forms of nonconsensual sexual contact (Koss, Gidycz, and Wisniewski 1987, 163). *Ms. Magazine* sounded the alarm, publishing a book-length examination of the data, *I Never Called It Rape: The Ms. Report on Recognizing, Fighting and Surviving Date*

and Acquaintance Rape (Warshaw 1988). The title acknowledged the reality that while sexual violence was common among
college students, appropriate language was often out of reach.
Because campus rape "looked" different than the stereotypical
stranger-in-the-bushes archetype, survivor agency to claim the
violation as rape was severely restricted. Katie Koestner, who survived rape as a first-year student at the College of William and
Mary in 1991, publicly disclosed her experiences to both the
media and to officials of the institution. Koestner was subjected
to extensive harassment by her peers and inaction by the school's
administrators (Gibbs 1991). Koestner's case became iconic in
the history of the campus antirape movement and the phenomenon of "date rape." She represented not only a survivor of rape
who was terribly mistreated by her institution but one who
was willing to defy the stigma and speak out openly and confidently about her experience (Koestner 2000, 35–37). Prob-
lematically, those who have greatest access to media platforms
and are accorded the most public empathy, are often white,
heterosexual women (Harris 2019, 8).

SEXUAL VIOLENCE ACTIVISM: STUDENTS MOBILIZE

Though community-based activism protesting sexual violence
in the United States was alive and well in the 1970s, media coverage made more visible the mobilizing against sexual violence
on campuses in the late 1980s and proliferated in the 1990s
(Gold and Villari 2000, 6–10). The renewed attention to
women's bodily integrity, sometimes called the "sex wars,"
emerged during this time. Student agitation kicked up after a
period of relative abeyance of all kinds of student activism during the Reagan years (Altbach and Cohen 1990, 32). The term

*date rape** became the phrase of choice for those confronting sexual violence on campuses. Administrators blamed alcohol and the aura of permissiveness ushered in with co-ed dormitories (Celis 1991, A1). Student activists were becoming more attuned to ways that institutions provided or neglected to provide structural support for survivors.

This attunement, in some cases, led to strong advocacy. For example, at the University of Minnesota, students organized a vocal protest and petition drive in support of the sexual violence resource center program director who advocated (against the director) to allow students to be actively involved in the work of counseling and advising peers (Driessen 2020, 572). Advisor Susan Villari and then-activist Jodi Gold, editors of one of the earliest books documenting student activism against sexual assault, founded Students Together Acting Against Rape (STAAR) at the University of Pennsylvania in 1989 and later hosted the first conference of Speak Out: The North American Student Coalition Against Sexual Violence (Gold 2000, xviv). Describing the 1990s as a "national chat room on sex, violence, equality and power" (p. xiii), Gold and her compatriots were slowly coming to terms with the knowledge that, if colleges were to become violence free, students were going to have to exert their activist power and press colleges and universities to change.

The activism fomented in the 1990s did not happen in a vacuum. For the first time in its history, the federal government began to take serious notice. Senator Joseph Biden of Delaware introduced the Violence Against Women Act (VAWA) of 1990, which was signed into law in 1994. Passed in 1993, Title IV of

---

* Feminists have critiqued the term *date rape* as problematic, as it somehow lessens the offense by associating it with being on a date. For more on this, see Moore 2011.

this act specifically "authorize[d] the Secretary of Education to make, on a competitive basis, grants to and contracts with institutions of higher education for rape education and prevention programs" (United States Congress 1993). Federal money began to pour into colleges and universities to make system-wide efforts to combat sexual and domestic violence, primarily focusing on police training and counseling and medical care for survivors. Students, savvy about the impact a large federal grant could play in shifting the conversation about sexual violence on campus, began pressuring their campus officials to apply for these federal grants. Recognizing they were ill-equipped to meet the federal regulations without additional funding, many colleges and universities pursued this funding, which was instrumental in building the earliest campus-based support services for survivors (Butler et al. 2019). The growing momentum and visibility of the North American Coalition of Students Against Sexual Assault enabled student activists to compare tactics and outcomes across geographic and institutional differences.

Around the same time, survivors of sexual violence at Brown University began writing the names of their rapists on bathroom walls at the Ivy League university (Schwartz 1990). A coalition of students called BASH (Brown Against Sexual Harassment) began organizing to defend the rights of the women to do so, decrying the lack of survivor-friendly policies and procedures for redress at the institution. Importantly, students (including Jesselyn Alicia Brown) at Brown resorted to writing on stalls only after they sought redress through official channels and were largely ignored. Together with three other students whose cases had been summarily dismissed by administrators with no real consequences for the perpetrators, Jesselyn Brown formed the Committee of Four to attempt to effect change with the administrators (Brown 2000, 83–84). The university set up a separate grievance process to protect the rights of men named on bathroom stall graffiti, demonstrating the right to free speech was not ensured when exercised by women in response to faulty bureaucratic systems. While no single incident launched all activism on college campuses, the media attention spotlighting the guerilla activism at Brown and the subsequent embarrassment faced by administrators at Brown and other high-profile institutions marked the end of students' passive acceptance of institutional indifference to sexual violence (Heldman, Ackerman, and Breckenridge-Jackson 2018, 34).

Activists were not alone in addressing sexual violence in this era. Katie Roiphe (who earned a PhD from Princeton in 1995) authored *The Morning After: Sex, Fear, and Feminism on Campus* (1993), a polemic against the growing awareness of campus rape and the resultant activism. Roiphe declared the campus antirape movement hysterical, noting the fascination of activists with rape and their mistaken portrayals of women as innocent victims and men as predators. Amplified by conservative pundits and media outlets clamoring for the chance to deaden the ardor of student activists, Roiphe obfuscated the many complex issues concerning campus sexual violence. Belying its effectiveness, Roiphe's argument centered on a specific critique of activism. As Lacey (1994) noted, "Roiphe is contemptuous of group action and public experiences; she claims 'the individual power of each story is sapped by the collective mode of expression'" (636).

The conservative backlash notwithstanding, activism against sexual violence continued relatively consistently throughout the 1990s and was emboldened once again when scholars began asserting inadequate campus sexual violence policies could be a violation of Title IX (Klein 2018, 71). Feminist legal scholar Catherine MacKinnon was first to name sexual harassment in the workplace settings as a violation of Title VII, the federal law designed to ensure equal employment opportunity for men and women in 1979 (MacKinnon 1979). A landmark case in 1992 (*Franklin v. Gwinnet County Public Schools*) paved the way for victims to hold educational institutions accountable in a fiduciary sense after experiencing harassment (Harris 2019, 6).

The upsurge in campus activism continued through the last decade of the twentieth century. At Harvard University, a student arrested for committing sexual violence against a fellow student eluded public notice until he plead guilty to six felony charges in district court. When Harvard students were made aware of the incident by the student-led Coalition Against Sexual Violence (CASV), they protested in the hundreds outside the administration building with signs reading "Rape Happens at Harvard" (Heller 1999). Critical of Harvard's inadequate policies and fumbling on issues of evidence and testimony, CASV used a variety of strategies, including enlisting a student to file an Office of Civil Rights complaint against the institution and collaborating with high-profile civil rights attorneys to apply public pressure for their cause (Heineman 2000).

SURVIVOR ACTIVISM:
VISIBLE, VOCAL, VALUABLE

As noted in the beginning of this chapter, survivors of sexual violence have been especially impactful in raising visibility and awareness of campus sexual violence activism. Survivors are in a unique position to draw from personal experience to elicit sympathy from a broader public, including but not limited to peers on their own campuses.

This overview of the history of movements to end sexual violence belies the fact that campus sexual violence is a problem much older than the movements to end it. The fact that elite men's colleges in New England ran buses back and forth between their campuses and the local women's colleges in the 1950s—colloquially called "fuck trucks" (Sheidlower 2009, 167)—points to the reality that college women's bodies and sexual agency have long been viewed and positioned as the purview of the men who desire them. Additionally, for most of the history of higher education in this country, LGBTQ+ college students were routinely disciplined or expelled for expressing queer desire, a practice that inevitably pushed their dating lives and sexual subcultures underground, making them vulnerable to victimization (Marine 2011, 12). These are the realities of campus sexual culture that inarguably contributed to the occurrence of sexual violence long before a group of deeply committed students at the University of Pennsylvania occupied their campus administration building in protest of inadequate rape policy in 1973 (Gold and Villari 2000, 6).

Like all social movements, the movement to end campus sexual violence continues to evolve, to reinvent itself, and to adapt to the shifting winds of local, state, and federal policymaking. It continues to adapt to the changes in normative understandings of the "why" of rape: "no means no," "affirmative consent," and all other permutations. Campus sexual violence activism continues to stand and resist the notion that rape is just something that is going to happen to some students in college. Campus sexual violence activists continue to demand safe campuses and to raise their collective voices until campuses are free of sexual violence. They continue to work across boundaries of identity and political difference and to swim against the tide of mainstream peer apathy regarding the urgency of their cause, ever toward the goal of a violence-free world (Lewis and Marine 2018).

How can we avoid repeating history? Given the work of activists of the past, several questions inspired this book: What can we learn from the stories of those who enact this resistance, this insistence, in the twenty-first-century #MeToo movement? What do campus sexual violence activists have to say to their peers, to student affairs practitioners, and to their institutional leaders? What do they help us understand about what remains to be done?

Chapter 2

THE LANDSCAPE OF TWENTY-FIRST- CENTURY STUDENT SEXUAL VIOLENCE ACTIVISM

Sexual violence activism in the twentieth century took a variety of forms, and activists engaged a variety of constituencies (feminists, other survivors, and lawmakers, principally) to advance their cause. Initiated by Women of Color and later led by others, these movements were diverse in their goals and approaches, and in many locales, were more community based than campus based. To fully understand the contours of sexual assault activism in the first quarter of the twenty-first century, there are two important contexts to identify.

First is the local context in which student activists are working—the institutional culture, recent events related to administrative response of sexual violence, and the students' perception of power brokers and levers to push toward change. A second relevant context is the larger national context of neoliberal encroachment within higher education, politics and policy changes related to Title IX and other federal initiatives, and the students' sense of how these factors were impinging on or advancing their work. Both contexts mattered enormously to the campus sexual violence activists in our study and shaped the ways they spoke about and formulated action plans. In many cases, the local contexts bled into the national, as the high-profile nature of institutional mishandling of cases became publicly known and written and talked about in the news. This often fueled the students' desire to enact change and inspired activists across disparate campus contexts. As a result, the work of CSVAs is interconnected and complementary. CSVAs across the country are ideologically and strategically aligned.

To provide greater clarity on the ways that local and national contexts simultaneously informed the work of activists in this book, we will weave that tapestry more visibly. What happened in the first two decades of the twenty-first century that inevitably shaped and catalyzed student activism to end sexual violence? In this chapter, we take a closer look at the *why* of this moment: naming the levers bearing on student activists in ways that are prompting them to action, and what we know about the nature of the work and its impact. College student activism has certainly surged in the last decade (Linder et al. 2019c, 528; Marine and Lewis 2019, 886), as has social science research on sexual violence activism. With each successive decade, student activists find new and more compelling reasons to organize and to take to the campus streets. A combination of factors and social forces are responsible for the uptick in students' mobilization against campus sexual violence. Neoliberalism in the modern university context has created a backdrop that depersonalizes and commodifies the college experience. Additionally, recent changes in the application of Title IX to the adjudication of sexual violence, the proliferation of activist organizations dedicated to amplifying survivor voices and concerns, the confluence of student activism alongside national and international movements such as #MeToo and #TimesUp, and the ongoing and rampant mismanagement of college adjudication policies have impacted campus activism in the last 20 years, and yet, despite decades of implemented prevention programs, the incidence and prevalence of sexual violence on campuses have remained unchanged (Harris and Linder 2017, xi). Taken together, these factors have created a set of conditions for an upsurge in campus sexual violence activism, with survivor and student activists actively pressing campus and national leaders and for change.

NEOLIBERALISM IN THE CONTEMPORARY UNIVERSITY

Among other changes that contribute to conditions ripe for activism is the relatively recent encroachment of neoliberalism in the modern US college and university. Neoliberalism "refers to the policies and processes whereby a relative handful of private interests are permitted to control as much as possible of social life in order to maximize their personal profit" (Giroux 2002, 425). Within the contemporary American university, these policies and processes manifest in numerous ways, including a

hyperfocus on achievement via competition, prioritizing practices that maximize profit, fostering policies that position universities favorably in rankings, and assessing scholars' merits
based on quantifiable productivity. Neoliberalism has shaped
campus climate and culture in innumerable ways, but perhaps
most relevant to the topic of this book by depersonalizing the
experiences of college students, particularly those that are traumatic, and eschewing consideration of anything that detracts
from an institution's reputation (Piller and Cho 2013, 27). A
focus on reputation demands that institutions, and those who
lead them, refuse engagement with anything that casts the university in a negative light, particularly when it is defined by the
messiness of human behaviors and emotions that accompany
violence (Marine and Lewis 2020). Because neoliberalism centers the victor, those who identify as victim are unsettling and
thus are disregarded (Prior and de Heer 2021, 6). Since the
1980s, scholars have documented the invidious effects of neoliberalism in higher education and have suggested that it has
taken hold across all domains of higher education (Bottrell
and Manathunga 2018). Neoliberalism thus permeates the
ways that campus leaders think about, engage (or refuse engagement with), and regard sexual violence survivors, and side-
step responsibility for addressing the systemic manifestations of
toxic masculinity such as sexual violence (Hill and Naik 2021,
280). In the absence of a commitment toward systemic change,
sexual violence proliferates, and college campuses become, in
turn, hotbeds for student dissatisfaction and unrest.

TITLE IX: PANACEA OR PERIL?

Title IX (or as it is formally known, Title IX of the Education
Amendments of 1972) has been adopted for use in the fight

against campus sexual violence and harassment* for the last two decades. The advent of Title IX as a remedy for sexual harassment and sexual violence has undoubtedly broadened discourse about the forms of access and opportunity that students, especially women and transgender and nonbinary students, are entitled to. Bunny Sandler's impetus to develop the law emanated from a clear sense that women were denied full participation in education through the existing civil rights legislation (such as Title VII and the Civil Rights Act) (Fitzgerald 2020). The law advanced the notion that penalizing colleges financially for discrimination would be essential to ending it (Sandler 1981, 53). The law has been leveraged for numerous egalitarian ends since it was passed, ensuring full participation for women and girls, and in some cases transgender students, in all educational arenas. While it is typically associated with advancing women's participation in athletics, it has been used to many different forms of both subtle and flagrant gender discrimination both in primary and secondary schools, colleges, and universities (Melnick 2018, 4–6).

While the federal government is deeply implicated in the enforcement of college and university sexual violence policy today, it wasn't until the early 1990s that Title IX was thought of as a remedy to address sexual harassment and violence on campus as well. In 1987 Congress passed the 1987 Civil Rights Restoration Act, which affirmed that failure to remedy any Title IX violation reported to an institution would jeopardize an institution's federal educational funding (Graham 1998, 415–416). It was a survivor (Steinberg 1991, 52) who first named the reality

---

* Throughout this chapter, we use the terms *sexual harassment* (the term of choice in the Title IX statute, and throughout the May 2020 regulations) and *sexual violence* (the term more commonly used by higher education researchers) interchangeably.

that rape must be considered an extreme form of sexual harassment. Steinberg noted that in *Lipsett v. University of Puerto
Rico,* the plaintiff was subjected to repeated and increasingly
severe forms of sexual harassment during her training as a
medical resident. As a medical resident, Lipsett was considered
both an employee of the university and a student. Sufficient evidence of a hostile work environment was presented to support
the allegation that supervising faculty failed to investigate Lipsett's complaints. Under Title IX, the decision in the case rested
on the requirement that an educational institution is liable for
any misconduct performed by a supervisor and can be held accountable for harassment. *Lipsett v. University of Puerto Rico* effectively set the precedent for institutional accountability and
in some cases financial redress going forward.

Institutional accountability for Title IX–related misconduct
was somewhat elusive until the establishment of a federal oversight body to conduct investigations of reported infractions. In
1997 the Clinton administration announced the first guidance
regarding the application of Title IX to campus sexual harassment and violence. The Office for Civil Rights (OCR), under
the auspices of the Department of Education, would be the primary oversight body to address violations in compliance
(United States Department of Education Office for Civil Rights
1997). From that moment, the work of numerous women's
rights advocates pushing for institutional accountability on sexual violence and sexual harassment was vindicated, and the
long crusade to hold institutions accountable began in earnest.

Numerous lawsuits against colleges thought to be in violation of this policy proliferated during this period (Silbaugh
2015, 1053–1056). Attorney Wendy Murphy brought suit
against Harvard University in 2002 for requiring complainants
to provide "sufficient corroborating evidence" at the time of a

report of sexual assault for it to be adjudicated. Such requirements, Murphy argued, violated both the letter and the spirit
of the law, noting that "Harvard is the first school to put in writing that the word of a woman is not good enough" (Mehren
2002). In the same year, Tiffany Williams, a student at the University of Georgia, reported a rape she endured at the hands of
a star athlete, Tony Cole, and later sued for lack of redress. Williams's case shifted the burden for responding promptly and
effectively to institutions and raised the stakes as hefty punitive
damages were pursued (Walker 2010, 98).

In 2006 amplified anxiety about compliant usage of Title IX
to address sexual violence, the result of a significant uptick in
violations reported to the OCR, resulted in the release of the
first of several subsequent "Dear Colleague" Letters (DCLs).
The DCLs were designed to further clarify the roles and responsibilities of educational institution officials responding to sexual
harassment (Monroe 2006). Despite pressure from activists to
expand Title IX's coverage to those experiencing sex-based harassment as LGBTQ+ people, the 2006 DCL refused to do so.
Two years later, an OCR-issued pamphlet entitled *Sexual Harassment: It's Not Academic* acknowledged that many incidents of
harassment rise to the level of a criminal (police) report but did
not absolve the institution's responsibility to thoroughly investigate and respond to harassment (United States Department
of Education Office for Civil Rights 2008).

The years that followed the inauguration of President Barack
Obama in 2009 saw the most significant increase yet in federal
commitment to enforcing Title IX's requirements vis-à-vis college
sexual assault. Together, Obama and Vice President Joseph R.
Biden—the leading senate proponent of the first Violence
Against Women Act, first passed in 1994—crafted and actively promoted the It's On Us (using the hashtag #ItsOnUS)

campaign. The campaign was anchored by a comprehensive web resource that touted evidence-based practices, including bystander intervention programs, culturally responsive prevention education, and targeted programs for student athletes (It's On Us 2020). The website signaled the administration's interest in setting a tone, building a culture of support for survivors and accountability for perpetrators, a bold and important move away from only proposing more policy initiatives.

While the Obama-era DCLs and the #ItsOnUS campaign reflected progress since 1998 in instantiating institutional obligations, such efforts were not, in fact, a panacea. While these were positive additions to the commitment of federal leadership on this issue, policy violations reported to the OCR increased from 9 in 2009 to 102 in 2014, indicating both increased awareness and, likely, the ongoing and rampant mishandling of cases (New 2015). The 2011 DCL, widely viewed as the most comprehensive and strident to date, set expectations for institutional leaders to respond to sexual harassment happening on or off college and university campuses (as opposed to previous such memoranda, which focused equally on K–12 schools). The letter required the appointment of a trained and visible coordinator for Title IX issues and shifted the burden of responsibility toward a "preponderance of evidence" standard as opposed to the "clear and convincing" evidentiary standard used in many college processes at the time (Ali 2011). But perhaps most significantly, this 2011 DCL was the first to boldly name failure to comply as attended by significant penalties. Conservative groups around the country, such as the Foundation for Individual Rights in Education (FIRE), perceived the letter to have a chilling effect on academic freedom and institutional autonomy, and decried it (Creeley 2011). Colleges and university leaders, however, largely set to work meeting the requirements to ensure avoidance of the dreaded two-word specter: OCR lawsuit.

The administration's final commentary regarding campus sexual violence was the release of the 2016 DCL, which clarified the application of Title IX to the protection, support, safety, and flourishing of transgender students in educational institutions (Lhamon and Gupta 2016, 2–3). While the use of Title IX to address sexual harassment was not a panacea during this period, its use certainly ensured that the issue of campus sexual violence remained on the agenda of the federal government. In the absence of Title IX, colleges and universities were left to their own devices, and to the whims of their state and district courts' interpretations of responsibility and liability. Importantly, the progress made was primarily thanks to relentless advocacy by researchers and activists in the movement, starting with Bunny Sandler, and not politicians.

While some expressed reservations about investing in a federal law as the remedy for deeply entrenched and toxic cultures (Harris and Linder 2017, 9; Yung 2015, 893), others hailed the use of the law as an improvement and as a way to ensure colleges would take notice (Cantalupo 2012, 522–523; Harris 2019, 8; Tani 2016, 1869–1871; Wooten and Mitchell 2015). This of course depends on Title IX being properly and faithfully enacted by colleges and universities, increasing transparency, and promoting safer and more equitable environments. The decision to instantiate sexual harassment as a platform issue of one of the two major political parties in the United States was significant; however, in a matter of years a very different set of values and priorities would illustrate just how porous and malleable federal use of Title IX would be. Because the DCLs' guidance was not written into law, and because they did not have the scaffolding of regulation behind them, the letters were all too easy to dismiss when a very different and politically unsympathetic presidential administration took the helm in 2016.

THE TRUMP ADMINISTRATION AND TITLE IX ENFORCEMENT

The progressive policy enforcement in place in the federal government since 2009 came to an abrupt halt with the election of Donald J. Trump in 2016 (Bedera 2020). As one of her first acts of legislation empowerment, Trump's Secretary of Education Betsy DeVos moved to rescind the 2011 and 2016 DCLs, inciting what many saw as a needless national referendum on the issue (Joyce 2017). Taking advice and counsel from accused students and their families and men's rights groups, DeVos acted swiftly to suspend the previous guidance and cast doubt on their constitutionality. DeVos launched a long and arduous process of public comment, known as the *Notice of Proposed Rulemaking* (United States Department of Education Office for Civil Rights 2018), announcing her intentions to make changes to Title IX. The previous tone and spirit of the federal government's response was unapologetically survivor centered. But in contrast, the regulations now under DeVos's reconstruction displaced the focus on empowering survivors and lessening trauma in order to address perceived slights in due process (Kingkade 2018). College student activists, paying close attention to these developments, began to see firsthand the role that the federal government could and would play in advancing Title IX as a remedy to sexual violence on campus. Trump and DeVos's reframing of the law elicited a strong response from activists, who loudly sounded the alarm for what they cautioned would be a complete rollback of decades of progress (Brown 2017).

Acting as watchdogs of federal intervention on the issue since the late 1990s, national survivor advocacy organizations quickly mobilized and released public statements. Advocacy groups panned DeVos's actions and the tenor of the announcement, which centered on leveraging accusations of slipping due process in college adjudication processes (Kreighbaum 2019). Tapping into prominent newspapers, social media platforms, and the notoriety of high-profile women's rights attorneys, advocacy organizations such as Project Callisto, End Rape On Campus, and Know Your IX began to take up visible and vocal space in calling for the restoration of and further progress on Title IX to end campus sexual violence (Clark 2018, 103).

ACTIVIST ORGANIZATIONS AND THE END OF SILENCE AND SHAMING

The visibility of survivor advocacy organizations signaled their importance as a second factor in the upsurge in student activism in the last decade. Since their emergence in the late 1990s, activist organizations dedicated to advancing survivor visibility while addressing an ongoing lack of accountability of colleges and universities to survivors have proliferated, building a steady presence in the landscape of public attention to this issue. These organizations play three roles: speaking out on matters of concern to survivors, providing resources to activists around the country, and bolstering the impact and visibility of activists in local/institutional settings. Often staffed on shoestring budgets by young and energetic former campus activists, these organizations' formidable impact has indelibly shaped the movement. Survivors have long endured being shamed and judged for their choices (Gold and Villari 2000). Their stories were doubted, and harassment and retaliation were commonplace (Gibbs 1991; Koestner 2000). By centering and uplifting survivor voices, and survivor primacy in the movement, leaders of these organizations resisted narratives of victim culpability and fragility, acting affirmatively to flip scripts of shame and hiding often forced on survivors (Heldman, Ackerman, and Breckenridge-Jackson 2018, 117–118).

Making victim-shaming an unacceptable practice is an up-hill battle in the midst of rape-supportive campus (and national) cultures (Staros 2018, 87–90). Publicly named survivors, such as Brittany Williams and Katie Koestner, who brought high-profile civil cases of the late 1990s and early 2000s, were questioned, deeply criticized, and considered fair game for character assassination (Tuerkheimer 2021, 15). In a national context known for both its sexual permissiveness and sexual puritanism (Reis 2012, 3–5), victim-shaming had become deeply normalized and was catalyzed by the platforms provided to so-called do-me feminists (Ferriss and Young 2006, 90), who depicted survivors as attention-seeking and possibly delusional. Princeton graduate Katie Roiphe's 1994 book, *The Morning After: Sex, Fear, and Feminism* was especially vicious in its portrayal, referring to students at a Take Back the Night March in quotation marks ("survivors"), declaring that, as they share their stories, "they blur together in [her] mind," and explicitly doubting the veracity of their accounts (30, 31–42). Roiphe, Camille Paglia (1992), and other pundits caricatured survivors and their experiences (as well as the activists supporting them) as unhinged, taking over college campuses and elevating the crime rate with specious reports for no defensible reason.

The movement to reclaim and recenter the narrative in favor of survivors was gradual but powerful in the Trump era. An additional factor in this pendulum shift was the Oscar-nominated documentary *The Hunting Ground* (Dick and Ziering 2015). As the first feature-length film to center activist voices and to make the work they are doing more legitimate, Dick and Ziering's (2015) film not only portrayed the deep harm caused by institutional betrayal but humanized those working to change it. The documentary featured Annie Clark and Andrea Pino and traced their journey from surviving sexual violence at the University of North Carolina to building a nationwide network of survivors and their advocates to respond to ongoing negligence at colleges and universities (Dick and Ziering 2016; Pryal 2018).

Not everyone in *The Hunting Ground* was a professional activist, however. Kamillah Willingham, a student at Harvard Law School who came forward about being assaulted by a fellow student, risked losing a highly profitable and prestigious legal career by making her case public in the film. The film included the stories of dozens of survivors and was widely shown in college classrooms and movie theaters. While it has not been free of controversy (Soave 2015), the film established a widespread and long-standing narrative of institutional negligence and betrayal. Institutions were culpable for significant student trauma and suffering, an exposure that served to bolster activist movements and advancement of their messages and concerns. Suddenly whole areas of survivor experience that were previously off-limits, such as the experience of naming a perpetrator who is a well-known Division I athlete, naming institutional officials who were indifferent or hostile, and staging a press conference to name a class action suit of multiple survivors, became more commonplace. Prominent feminist attorneys, such as Gloria Allred, staged professional press conferences and invited national news media, bringing heightened attention to the issues (Grinberg 2014). In each of these cases, survivor organizations, amplified first by *The Hunting Ground's* exposure and amplified by national press coverage, meaningfully increased the visibility of survivors. It also revealed a thoughtful and strategic sophistication in activist strategies. Sexual violence activists were no longer simply individual women working for change on their individual campuses. Now they were creating broad, diverse, cross-institutional networks powered by clear messaging that were highly strategic. What began as a grassroots, campus-by-campus effort bloomed into a nationally visible network of activist organizations. The groups were bolstered by the platform of very visible allies, including wealthy and connected Hollywood celebrities.

#METOO AND #TIMESUP: THE DRUMBEAT SWELLS

In addition to the progress made by Title IX reform and the diligent grassroots work of survivor-led national advocacy organizations, survivor uprisings beyond the college campuses further promoted campus activism. The most prominent of these movements was the Twitter-based phenomenon known as #MeToo (Bogen et al. 2019, 8261). Tarana Burke, a survivor, activist, and founder of an organization started to support teen sexual abuse survivors, was the first to use the phrase "me too" in a post on the former social media platform MySpace in 2006 (Pellegrini 2018, 63). In her essay, she spoke of her assailant openly and her experiences with trauma, using the hashtag "MeToo" to indicate the ubiquity of the issue. The hashtag was picked up and advanced by actor Alyssa Milano in a 2017 tweet, quickly becoming viral and launching a nationwide movement with millions of women and other survivors claiming the hashtag. Media analysts have noted that celebrities, especially women actors, received the most retweets, as did others who were assaulted by well-known white men (Chou 2018). Thus, while the visibility of those claiming the hashtag was unevenly distributed, the impact of #MeToo has been described as groundbreaking (Mendes, Ringrose, and Keller 2018). While #MeToo was not a college-survivor-focused movement, inevitably many college survivors connected to and linked up with the movement, using it as the platform to amplify their voices (Hartocollis 2019).

A companion movement came about in the same time period and was known as #TimesUp. In 2018 a celebrated movie producer, Harvey Weinstein, was publicly named for his culpability in victimizing a number of women in Hollywood and was charged with criminal sexual predation (McKinley 2018). Weinstein, one of the wealthiest and most powerful men in Hollywood, wielded a great amount of control over casting and production. When several well-known actors came forward to name him as their assailant, the consequences were immediate and explosive. A group of 300 actors (mostly women) and other insiders in the film industry borrowed and started using #TimesUp to indicate not only the violence perpetrated by Weinstein but also the ongoing and widespread harassment and violence present in their industry and beyond. Importantly, the founders of the movement sought to deflect criticism of their rarified circumstances by strategically promoting fundraising and legal advocacy for less privileged women impacted by sexual abuse, including farmworkers (Buckley 2018).

While not directly linked to college women or college policy concerns, inevitably the widespread messaging of #MeToo and #TimesUp rendered it highly visible and accessible to college-age students and especially survivors. While activists in this book rarely named either #MeToo or #TimesUp as directly influencing their work, several noted the impact of hashtag activism: the resemblance akin to the "everywhereness" of surviving trauma (Howell and Itkowitz 2016, 33). Virtually every activist who participated in our study acknowledged the impact on their psyches of surviving trauma and how thinking about the work they wanted to do to end sexual violence was all encompassing. The effectiveness of these movements lay in their promise to resist victim shaming and turn the shame on perpe-trators. The allure of holding bad actors publicly accountable may have bolstered student activist resolve, but most sexual vio-lence activism seeks to transform culture and not simply hold perpetrators accountable (Marine and Lewis 2020, xii).

THE RAMPANT MISMANAGEMENT OF ADJUDICATION PROCESSES

The use of Title IX as a remedy for campus sexual violence changed the playing field for activists, because it meant that real costs (both fiduciary and reputational) would accrue to the most blatant offenders. In 2014 the OCR created and widely pro-moted a publicly accessible database for the tracking of re-ported offenses of Title IX, and for the first time, activists and the public at large could check and monitor the status of cases and their outcome (United States Department of Education 2014). As the number of reported violations crept up follow-ing the Obama administration's commitment to the issue, and despite a redoubling of resources, the Office of Civil Rights in-vestigation process regularly spanned months and, in some cases, years. This frequently left colleges (and those who lead them) in limbo regarding their culpability for adopting faulty, slow, or otherwise insufficient practices.

The database played an important role in advancing activ-ist work. Soon, an avalanche of stories in the popular media about the various ways that campus adjudication processes were mishandled, their outcomes bungled, and survivors being mis-treated began to proliferate. These reports spanned the globe; indeed, activist movements at campuses in the United Kingdom (Batty and Cherubini 2018), India (Anitha, Marine, and Lewis 2019), and South Africa (Draper 2019) all lent credence to the idea that colleges all across the world were falling short on the vital work of responding to sexual violence. In addition to the high-profile cases revealed and explored in *The Hunting Ground*, leaders at other prominent universities in the United States (including Stanford, MIT, and the University of California at Berkeley) were accused of exhibiting indifference or hostility to survivors and mishandling complaints, both in the court of public opinion and by the Office of Civil Rights (Felch and Song 2014; Kadvany 2018). While the outcomes (and penalties) varied widely, the outcomes of these cases consistently revealed that colleges were failing to fully comply with federal requirements, prompting activists to recognize that any problems happening in their local contexts likely also had national implications. Many different kinds of adjudicatory malfeasance were named in these reported violations, ranging from significant lag times in conducting and concluding investigations to allegations of inappropriate evidence collection. Students complained about noncompliant procedures in the hearing room, in the deliberations, and in allegations of light sanctioning. In a particularly egregious and attention-getting case, a $70 million class action lawsuit against Dartmouth College, alleging multiple unaddressed instances of sexual violence and harassment emanating from the Department of Psychological and Brain Sciences toward both graduate and undergraduate students, merited its own press conference with celebrity attorney Gloria Allred at the center of the dispute (Hartcollis 2019). The case was settled out of court in 2019 and resulted in nine former and current students receiving $14 million in damages (Flaherty 2019). The reverberations of the Dartmouth case served as a stark reminder of the ways that even powerful and well-resourced universities were vulnerable and subjected to humiliation attendant to poorly constructed reporting mechanisms. Alumni and student activists at Dartmouth joined together under the mantle of an organization (and hashtag) named #DartmouthDoBetter and referred to the settlement as gratifying (Hartocollis 2019).

Importantly, accused students also stepped forward to file reported violations of Title IX protections for them, a phenomenon that only increased in the years following the change in administrations from more (Obama) to less (Trump) progressive (Jesse 2019). Principal among the strategies of accused students were efforts to discredit the adjudication boards tasked with making a decision regarding responsibility. In an early case of alleged bias of a hearing board against an accused student (*John Doe v. Brandeis*), the student (and his attorney) alleged that the mere presence of training for the conduct board—training that included definitions and descriptions of common responses to trauma among rape survivors—introduced bias into the proceedings (United States District Court 2016). Similarly, a student at Columbia alleged that the hearing board found him responsible for sexual misconduct largely in part to the fact that he was male (Volokh 2016). Jameis Winston, the Florida State quarterback accused of rape in 2012 by a fellow student (a case prominently featured in *The Hunting Ground*), took a different tack, countersuing his accuser for defamation and calling her accusations "willful, malicious and false" (Tracy 2015). Later, the case was settled out of court. Erica Kinsman, who accused Winston of rape, settled out of court for unspecified damages, and Florida State University paid Kinsman $950,000 in damages and agreed to improve its education, prevention, and response mechanisms in reply to a lawsuit she filed against the institution (Florida State University 2016).

The cumulative effect of embarrassing, costly, and widely reported lawsuits—both within the Office of Civil Rights and in local, state, and district courts around the country—represented a meaningful shift in the power dynamic related to sexual violence, a shift that did not go unnoticed by activists and advocacy organizations. Following several decades of shame-induced silencing of survivors and their supporters, the voices and plights of survivors were beginning to resonate with juries, with the media, and most importantly, with activists.

SURVIVOR-ACTIVISTS IN THE #METOO MOVEMENT

Three specific examples of survivor activism in the early twenty-first century illuminate the particular impact of survivor-based expression and the change that such expression can and does hasten.

Emma Sulcowicz, a former student at Columbia University (2011–2015), engaged in a multimonth performance art project in which she carried the mattress where she was raped around campus to all classes, events, and activities she took part in for 14 months. The performance, entitled Carry That Weight, was intended to be a visual reminder of the daily struggle of living with trauma after an experience with sexual harm (Mitra 2015). It was dually intended, Sulcowicz stated, to remind viewers that "the system is broken because it is so much based on proof that a lot of rape survivors don't have" (Bazelon 2015).

In another high-profile case, Wagatwe Wanjuki filed a Title IX complaint against Tufts University in 2009 after she was expelled from the university putatively for academic failure, a consequence of her rape trauma. Wanjuki wrote about the dismissal of her case in the Tufts adjudication process and bemoaned the profound insensitivity of Tufts administrators to whom she turned after her rape, referring to their tendency to treat rape as something to attend to on a compliance checklist (Wanjuki 2017, viii). Her rage regarding the mistreatment she suffered was encapsulated in her decision to light her Tufts sweatshirt on fire live on Facebook in 2016. Wanjuki's continued advocacy for intersectional, trauma-informed sexual violence response, and her coining of the hashtag #SurvivorPrivilege, have earned her a place among the current era's most visible activists (Kingkade 2014).

Survivor advocacy, often performed alone and without acclaim, is sometimes embodied by a group of survivors taking on the same institutional foe. For example, seven women, all survivors of sexual harassment and abuse, collectively brought a $70 million lawsuit against Dartmouth College after enduring egregious abuse by three faculty in the Department of Psychological and Brain Sciences. Press coverage of the lawsuit summarized the case: "The seven plaintiffs, each an exemplary female scientist at the start of her career, came to Dartmouth to contribute to a crucial and burgeoning field of academic study . . . Plaintiffs were instead sexually harassed and sexually assaulted by the department's tenured professors and expected to tolerate increasing levels of sexual predation" (Flaherty 2018).

As previously mentioned, the suit was eventually settled for $14 million and was accompanied by contrition from Dartmouth's President Philip Hanlon, who commented, "Through this process, we have learned lessons that we believe will enable us to root out this behavior immediately if it ever threatens our campus community again" (Hartocollis 2019).

In these three cases and others, the survivor-activists involved brought significant embarrassment to their institutions. Their stories resonated with so many survivors because, in each case, these survivors put a very human face and name to the deep suffering and loss they had endured. Their intentional and strategic use of messaging and media coverage allowed them to marshal visible and sustained support from peers, allies, public figures, and alumni. In turn, their visibility catalyzed institutional policy change through the twin levers of institutional embarrassment and the embodiment of raw survivor vulnerability.

As argued in this chapter, four distinct phenomena influenced the recent increase in sexual violence activism by college students across the country. First, the influential and visible evolution of Title IX as a remedy for campus sexual violence undoubtedly played a role in students' awareness and agitation for change. The gradual and progressive shift in the way Title IX was leveraged for change on campuses was abruptly halted in 2016 by the rescinding of the Obama-era DCLs and the guidance and norm-setting they represented (Kingkade 2018). The birth and growth of survivor-led, national advocacy organizations were additionally influential in catalyzing movement on campuses across the country; the organizations' emphasis on grassroots organizing, training, and collective action resonated strongly with activists at small colleges as well as those at massive research universities. And finally, the visibility of cases brought against institutions for malfeasance in the adjudication process revealed the vulnerability of institutions, and their susceptibility to impulsive pivots in the aftermath of negative public press. Each of these factors catalyzed movements to end sexual violence on numerous campuses across the country and mobilized activists to press for change against the many barriers of resistance and in many cases, indifference.

According to Jerusha O. Conner (2020), student activism has increased in the last decade as a result of other intersecting factors, including a resurgence of social studies curricula in schools, service learning, and civic engagement initiatives. Student activists find their way to causes, and to one another, and report deriving great meaning and reward in taking oppositional stances against power structures, and building strategies to effect change (Miller and Tolliver 2017). However, as scholars have shown, performing activist work requires intense emotional, cognitive, and relational energy from students and can significantly detract from their mental and physical well-being (Linder et al. 2019c, 536).

Activists fighting against sexual violence and sexual violence supportive cultures on their campuses are also required to fight an insidious stereotype that plagues the so-called millennial and Generation Z cohort: that of being privileged, coddled "snowflakes" and superficially self-righteous "social justice warriors," stereotypes that render them simultaneously aggressively strident and patently fragile (Pandit 2015). These tropes cast a shadow of ineffectiveness, and presumed naivete, over the highly committed and principled work they perform. These stereotypes interrupt the sincere and often highly strategic positions they assume and the transformation they so earnestly work to achieve.

Alternatively, in the age of social media–driven impression management and self-promotion, sexual violence activism can be understood as a legitimate co-curricular student activity. It could well be that the time CSVAs spend mobilizing a community to effect change can confirm and impact their career decisions and opportunities. Simultaneously, the protection of institutional brand representation on social media by neoliberally focused universities can foreclose CSVAs' efforts, consequently undermining the use-value of their personal or group social media feeds.

Colleges and universities are social institutions that are slow to change. Institutions, colleges, and universities pursue self-protection at all costs and often choose to dismiss the work and concerns of activists. The changework (Marine and Lewis 2020) ardently pursued by CSVAs nevertheless continues. This book seeks to better understand the visions of activists working to end sexual violence and to listen to their stories of activism.

Chapter 3

ACTIVIST IDENTITY, MOTIVATION, AND STRATEGIES

Unfortunately, it started with, in the same way it starts for a lot of other activists—having a very bad experience on campus, trying to go through the formal procedures to have these wrongs righted. And then realizing that the system doesn't work.

—Maya

I can't unlearn my trauma. I can't unlearn what's been done to me. So when I do this work I need everyone to understand that I do it because it's not necessarily like it's important to me. No, I have to do it to survive. I have to do it for the fact that generations of my family, my children and my children's children will have to keep doing this work if they want to survive. Eventually, maybe one day hopefully,

if I manifest it every night, we will live in a world where
we can take a break.
—Morgan

In our conversations with campus sexual violence activists, each shared with us their perspectives on why they engage in campus sexual violence activism, how they identify as CSVAs, and how they enact their activism on campus. They shared their strategies, articulated their motivation for CSV activism, and identified reasons why sexual violence activism is a meaningful and enduring commitment in their lives. Activists voiced their personal goals for activism and the changes needed in the culture and practices of their respective colleges and universities. CSVAs described ways their sexual violence activism affected them, positive and negative consequences for their academic progress, the souring of their campus peer relationships, and the development of a peer community through CSVA. Many activists shared how the stressful work to rid their campuses of sexual violence negatively impacted their mental health. But some also reflected on how they had personally grown from the experience and how their activism enabled their development as confident young adults.

Though all of the CVSAs mentioned the stresses of sexual violence activism, only a few survivor-activists and a few survivor-advocate activists mentioned that they had sought mental health counseling for their own trauma and/or the stress of sexual violence activism. Most CSVAs talked about how dedicating time, maintaining physical stamina, and staying mentally strong challenged their academic career and restricted their friendship groups to students who "want to fight the same system that you want to fight" (Morgan). The development of these friendship groups seemed central to activists' psychological well-being, and when coupled with professional therapeutic support, "the overwhelming amount of pressure" often felt by CSVAs was "definitely doable" (Eli). CSVA friendship groups, especially those constituted by other activists, seemed to function like traditional support groups, in which shared experience and empathy provide understanding and support for members. Similar to the way campus friendship groups form because of racial and gender anxiety and stresses, CSVA friendship groups serve as sites of self-empowerment, identity validation, and mental and emotional triage (Martínez-Alemán 2000).

Some activists like Eli and Danu shared that their academic performance suffered as a result of the time and energy spent on activism, but they reasoned that the goals and purposes of their activism (e.g., improving institutional support for survivors, survivor advocacy and campus education) outweighed academic performance. Morgan likened the focused energy directed at their activism to "a runner's high" that is sustained throughout the ups and downs of activism:

> It's like a runner's high. Right before that happens you kind of feel like "I'm gonna die" and then you're gonna crash and then you get another burst of [energy] . . . all of us were operating like go go go go go, kind of hit that crash, then start again . . . then like you know kind of plateaus and then go again and now you're like refocusing on how do you support survivors outside of institutions and then you go again.

In sum, campus sexual violence activism is a prevailing experience that has a bearing upon activists' sense of self, their health, and their mental well-being. Engagement with sexual violence activism is simultaneously exhausting and inspiring, isolating and socially engaging, empathic and self-empowering for CSVAs. Acutely conscious of dominant gender and racial discourses that inform campus culture, their assessments of institutional responses to sexual violence are testimony to administrative indifference to their activism, and effectual silencing of their voices.

WHY CAMPUS SEXUAL VIOLENCE ACTIVISM?

The CSVAs who shared their experiences, viewpoints, feelings about their activism, and its value and significance for their campuses revealed activist identities that were unequivocally rooted in their motivation to validate their own survivor experiences and to support and seek institutional amends for survivors of sexual violence. In what can be characterized as "identity-based activism" (Linder et al. 2019b, 43) their relationship to *surviving*—either as survivors of sexual violence themselves, or with their close relationships with friends or loved ones who are survivors—is the singularly salient source of motivation for most of these activists and a fundamental element of their identities as CSVAs.

SURVIVOR-ACTIVISTS

Among the activists, 10 identified as survivors of sexual violence, while a few alluded to being survivors. Some, like Nadia, experienced sexual violence before arriving in college, and through activism with other survivors began to "process" an experience that was still "fresh and raw and very difficult to try to process on [her] own." CSVA Nylah, at Howard University, is a survivor of campus-based sexual violence. At Howard University, a private, historically Black research university in Washington, DC, Nylah has actively protested survivor mistreatment of sexual assault and, together with other students and alumni of

Howard University, involved herself in a sexual violence awareness movement on social media that included the "Black Survivors Healing Fund" on GoFundMe.

Like Nylah, Maya is a survivor of campus-based sexual violence. Maya's observation that her identity as a CSVA began with her own sexual assault experience echoed those of other CSVAs whose identity as survivors anchored and inspired their activism. CSVAs who identified as survivors recognized that their activism was animated by and helped them to make sense of their sexual violence experiences. Activism helped them situate their own experience with sexual violence in the larger context of misogyny and not as their own isolated and traumatic experience. The active engagement with activism enabled survivor-activists to more fully grasp the effects of their own sexual assault and begin to deal with their own pain and trauma. As Morgan shared, by doing CSVA work, they were able to see that their sexual assault "story" did not mean that they were "not just another statistic," but it did mean that they had to experience a "kind of retraumatizing" that "brought up a lot of things that [they] hadn't yet dealt with." While at Harvard University, Danu understood that, as a survivor engaged in sexual violence activism she had "baggage" that had to be shared in peer community events on sexual violence. For others like Kayla, activism prompted a self-reckoning of their identity as a survivor, and though difficult, to claim ownership of that identity:

> Prior to organizing, I hadn't really even considered myself a survivor. It was like I knew I was assaulted and I've been assaulted on multiple occasions. However, it was very difficult for me to use that term and to feel as though it was something that represented me.

Like other survivor-activists, Kayla saw their survivor status as an organizing principle for their sexual violence activism. They are clear that their identity as a survivor composes their sense of self as an activist. Like all the other CSVAs who spoke with us, Kayla identified as someone who could engage in both affective and cognitive empathy. As a survivor and CSVA, Kayla's resolute empathy for other survivors of sexual violence is not independent from their ability to understand other survivor's perspectives and states of mind. Indeed, the shared status as survivors enabled CSVAs to compose identities that were not discrete but rather aspects of an integrated self. In Kayla's words:

> *I think going through the process of validating other people's experiences has almost forced me to be like, Okay, so I'm a survivor and what I've experienced isn't okay, and I deserve to have my story recognized the same way that I want every other survivor's story to be recognized. And that doesn't mean that like I should be the focal point, because . . . this is a collective issue . . . I would say the biggest thing I learned for myself was being able to validate my own experiences because a lot of people, especially people of color have been taught not to.*

CSVAs who are survivors of sexual violence appear to have an inner steadiness about who they are as survivors that serves as their internal framework for their activism. The survivor-activist component of their identities motivates their intentionality in SVA, clearly reflecting these salient aspects of their identities. It is important to note, however, that these CSVAs did not solely identify as survivor-activists, that is, they were clear about their many different social and cultural positionalities that are significant ingredients of their identities.

SURVIVOR ADVOCATES

CSVAs identify as activist-advocates for survivors of sexual violence. For many CSVAs, whether as survivors themselves or as advocates, being an advocate for others who have experienced sexual violence is a central feature of their identities as activists. CSVAs are guided by their commitment to other survivors, whether enacted through peer education and support or by challenging institutional practices and policies that reinforce misogynist norms or limit survivors' claims. As activists, they defend survivors by validating their claims, anxieties, and indignation. As survivor-activists, they understand themselves as empathic champions for survivors' care and affirmation. Yashica, a current student at Boston University, understood that her role or identity as a CSVA is as advocate and activist, that is, to be a source of support as well as a force for institutional change. Boston University is a private research university in Massachusetts. To raise awareness of the ongoing sexual violence around the campus, students at Boston University created the Campus Survivors Instagram page in 2020 for survivors of sexual violence to share their stories anonymously. Students also initiated the public art project titled, "I Will Walk with You" in 2016 for sexual violence prevention. Like other colleges and universities in Massachusetts, Boston University is required by the Commonwealth of Massachusetts to follow the guidelines set in the Every Voice Bill (Bill S. 764 Massachusetts Legislature). These guidelines, written collaboratively by the Every Voice Coalition (Boston students and survivors) and Massachusetts state legislators' sponsorship, enacted broad measures to support sexual assault survivors and students on any Massachusetts college or university (public or private) (Every Voice Coalition 2021).

Yashica understood that her role and identity as an activist are to "believe" survivors to work to enact change in her university:

Sometimes on our posts, there will be someone saying, "You are heard, I believe you." Even the words "I believe you" are so powerful because a lot of the time some people, their friends, don't believe them. Institutions don't believe them. You just feel completely disregarded. And you feel like people hear you but they don't "hear" you. And the comments are so supportive. I think our whole Instagram page is about supporting people and trying to bring them together and not only show that there is a problem, but also, we hope to, in the future, work towards preventing that problem, reducing it, and turn into something that's actively creating change in a system that needs it.

Activists like Anja and Coral are galvanized by the experience of others, often a woman close to them. Anja's support of a friend who had been sexually assaulted in the first week of college prompted her participation in Barnard-Columbia's No Red Tape sexual assault activism. A group of students at Barnard College at Columbia University has requested the university to allow the recording of the gender-based misconduct proceedings to be in line with the New York's anti–sexual violence bill (New York State Education Law, Senate Bill S5965, 2015) that calls for full transparency of the proceedings. After her mother's sexual assault in Coral's senior year and the lack of resources for sexual assault survivors, she committed herself to SVA when she enrolled in the University of California Irvine a year later. UCI is a public land-grant research university and participates in "Take Back the Night," where students, in solidarity with one another, unpack the impacts of power-based violence. Coral commented:

> *I decided to get involved in sexual assault activism in college. I wanted to start immediately. Like, right away I knew that I wanted to learn more about sexual assault and response to trauma and things around sexual assault, because my senior year of high school, my mom was sexually assaulted by a stranger. And in Fresno County, where I grew up, there aren't a whole lot of resources for survivors of sexual violence. There aren't a lot of resources for anyone in Fresno County. And it was really frustrating because, I mean, I was 17 and I didn't know how to help her. I had no idea what to do. I hated that feeling, that feeling of helplessness.*

Like Coral, Stanford University CSVA Subhadra's commitment is resolutely about service to survivors. Within the last few years, there has been a heightened awareness of campus rape culture at this private institution located in California. In 2020 Stanford Womxn in Law hosted its third annual Womxn March to protest the institutions' response to sexual violence and to show solidarity for global women's issues. The release of Stanford's 2019 Campus Climate Survey results found that nearly 40% of women experience sexual assault during their undergraduate education. Subhadra's pledge to serve survivors reflects this solidarity:

> *We're doing this for the next person who goes through sexual violence, hopefully doesn't have to, or if something happens, feels like they have a process they can trust to get*

justice. And part of that kind of is, if we're not doing this, who is? You can't trust the administration to always do the right thing.

Peer education programs and internships in campus women's centers often served as a critical means for their own development as activists. Coral, like many other CSVAs, engaged in peer education as one means to support survivors and enact campus change. Her identity as a CSVA is entwined with her experiences as a peer educator. Through her participation in the Campus Assault Resources and Education (CARE) office at UC Irvine, she educated herself and used this position to serve as an advocate for survivors. Alexia recognized that understanding "someone else's story" through peer education at the University of Maryland—in her case, dance performances—could educate the campus community about the trauma of sexual violence to ultimately legitimate survivor experience. At UCI, Anika acknowledged that her peer education efforts "started with just a lot of workshop and teachings" to "rally the Muslim students on campus" to engage with sexual violence activism but served to provide a public resource for Muslim survivors.

CSVAs recognized that the collaborative and intersectional nature of peer education programs energized their activism and was nourished by the collective character of neoactivism's intersectional character.

ACTIVIST IDENTITIES AND INTERSECTIONALITY

CSVAs' identities are informed by the politics of intersectionality. As Conner (2020) points out, present-day college activists are more apt to form coalitions and collaborations with a wide range of student identity-based groups than activists in the past. Today's sexual violence campus activists, like other campus activists, are engaged in broader concerns about social disparities and inequities that manifest on campus and appear to "transcend the confines of a narrow identity politics" common to previous generations of activists (Conner 2020, 5). The interconnected nature of social categorizations such as race, class, and gender, and the structures and discourses that have created and reinforce overlapping and interdependent systems of discrimination, are constitutive of activists' identities. CSVA's individual social locations and positionalities motivate their activism to revise sexual violence frameworks to make visible the ways in which sexual violence is connected to racism, homophobia, transphobia, and other discriminatory narratives.

As "neoactivists," CSVAs sought and valued campus intersectional coalitions (Conner 2020, 9). Conner describes neoactivists as "contemporary college student activists" who intentionally "link their social justice work" to previous generations' social activism (2020, 9). Today's neoactivism is set apart from conservative groups' campus activism by its "critical consciousness and intersectional perspective" (Conner 2020, 8). Both BIPOC- and white-identified CSVAs talked about how their intersectional social identities composed their identification and consequently informed their activist identity. BIPOC sexual violence activists like Nadia secure their CSVA identities to the intersectional reality of their experience:

I approach all of my work intersectionally. I value it tremendously and find it to be, frankly, non-negotiable if we're going to do this work. People's experiences with survivorship and then people's experience from police and police brutality and systemic racism, they don't exist in two separate spheres. They almost completely overlap in a lot of senses that one needs the other and the other needs the one.

The embodiment of racial and ethnic identifications is enormously meaningful in the development of CSVA identities. CSVAs know that their experience is marked by race and ethnicity, that bodies carry racial marginalization and subjugation.

Despite the prevalence of studies on campus sexual violence, most research studies lack racial and ethnic diversity (Zounlome et al. 2019, 873). However, in national data with representative samples, African American women do report higher rates of rape and sexual victimization than other racial and ethnic groups (Berzofsky et al. 2016, 3),* and the legacy of sexual violence among women in the United States is documented (Hobson and Young 2021). Researchers have found that among college women, sexual victimization is experienced by 36% of African American women and 26.3% of the white women (Gross 2006, 293). Sexual violence experienced by women is a historical trauma interrelated to their racialized and gendered oppression, a social status inextricably linked to slavery, and Morgan lives the reality that 20% of women are raped during their lifetimes (Institute for Women's Policy Research 2018). At the University of Maryland, Baltimore County (UMBC), a public research university located in Catonsville, Maryland, students stormed the UMBC administration building to confront their president on the institution's mishandling of sexual assaults of two UMBC students who were raped and had their reports ignored. The student activists created a list of demands and highlighted the need for the university to prioritize the safety of survivors. Confidently, Morgan explained:

> It's very important to me that everyone understands that part of my experience as an activist and as a survivor is

---

* The report suggests that the highest rates are among Native Indian / Alaskan Native women but caution that low sample sizes affect variance.

informed by my Blackness. It's informed by the fact that I
come into this work already knowing that if I don't do this
work, I'm just gonna be at risk.

Their gender identities, however, do not limit their understanding of their roles as CSVAs. Nadia believed that it is her awareness of her own intersectional identity that enhances her ability to understand that though the "trauma is different" for white, gender queer students, for example, it was shared trauma. Despite differences in social identities, Nadia enlisted the shared experience of surviving sexual violence to enact activism so that "it's not just going to work for people who look and live like [her]." It seems that being cognizant of and claiming their intersectional identities fuse CSVA identities to collective identities scripted by their socially marginalized and oppressed status. As a Muslim woman, for example, Anika views her role as a CSVA as doing "what [her] religion has preached to [her]" and that is to "care for all people."

Simultaneously, campus activists must also confront institutional racism along with misogyny, especially at predominantly white institutions (PWIs). Maya reflected that, as a woman of color at Georgetown, there "are a lot of straining things that occur especially when you're a Black woman or a woman of color working in this field." Georgetown University is a private, Catholic, Jesuit university in Washington, DC. In response to the changing legal context, the university is revising the processes for implementing Title IX and addressing sexual misconduct. Though Georgetown University has developed programs to create a survivor-centric campus environment, including a mandatory orientation program for first-year and transfer students on sexual violence, Maya was aware that there are "so many more barriers" to effect change on campus. She wondered if a more racially and ethnically diverse coalition of CSVAs would have been more effective.

At the State University of New York at Geneseo, a PWI campus that CSVA Emily describes as "whitewashed," sexual violence activism continues to be framed as a white women's concern despite efforts to acknowledge the intersectionality of sexual violence, and white activists' commitment to not speak for survivors of color. Emily and other CSVAs talked "at length about how race, gender, ethnicity, religion comes into play" but recognized that their own identities as "Christian white women" limited activism.

In contrast, at Middlebury College, a private liberal arts college in Middlebury, Vermont, and a PWI, Eli recognized that campus activism was discursively intersectional. Students at Middlebury College organized the "It Happens Here" (IHH) campaign by collecting stories and videos from student survivors and mapping the locations of incidents to raise awareness of sexual violence and to support survivors. Eli's identity as a CSVA was not in contrast to Middlebury's sexual violence activism that was "disproportionately queer, people of color," and in which "discourse around how people of color and people are affected differently by sexual violence was very present." Kayla's experience at Georgetown was similar to Eli's, but as was the case with all of the CSVAs, she thoughtfully engaged in a consideration of social identity and sexual violence:

> This past year I started really immersing myself a lot more within the community and finding a lot of community, especially with women and non-binary people, and truly, how it happened is through a lot of conversations with one another. And we started drawing a lot of connections with each other . . . It was becoming increasingly more than just

*like walking past each other on the street and saying 'hi' or
like ending up in the same place, it started to become a very
intentional attempt at trying to build community between
women and non-binary people on campus . . . There was
a group chat that was created called " girl magic" but it
did include non-binary people and through that group
chat, we all basically started airing out all of our grievances
with Title IX.*

At Stanford and Geneseo, however, sexual violence activists
are mostly "straight" and mostly white, and activists like Julia are
mindful that other students "who are also dealing with other
kinds of marginalization" should be part of the advocacy and
activism community.

CAMPUS CULTURE: THE INFLUENCE
OF ACADEMICS

Many CSVAs talked about the influence of academic work on
their identities as activists, including the study of gender, critical
race, intersectionality, and social movement theories. Through
academic coursework, campus activists like Andrea, an alumna
of the University of North Carolina, were exposed to social
and cultural theories that shape their identities as activists and
motivate their sexual violence activism. For Andrea, political science courses that exposed her to theories of "social movements,
in particular racial justice, gun violence, anti-smoking campaigns" enabled her to realize that sexual violence was "framed
as individual cases of sexual violence," when it is in fact an
identity-based social phenomenon. Moreover, through exposure
to these theories, Andrea realized that a sexual violence activism
strategy had to "combine the personal narrative" in an identity
politics framework. Andrea's exposure to feminist theories and

arguments presented in college and university courses, as for other CSVAs, facilitated the development of her consciousness about gender violence and administrative myopia. Her coursework and particular texts inspired her activism. For example, she recalled how reading feminist legal scholar Catharine MacKinnon's exposition on Title IX was "really profound" for her because it was through this exposition that she was able to see how Title IX was

> *about gender, it wasn't about sports, it wasn't about the administration, it was about [access to education] and how gender, the lack of support for students can lead to a lack of access to education.*

By studying MacKinnon's explanation of the discursive nature of gender discrimination in *Toward a Feminist Theory of State* (1989), Andrea was able to link gender violence to educational discrimination as central to administrative indolence. Julia, a Stanford University junior, recalled how early exposure to a course on sexual violence advocacy was "eye-opening." The instructor purposely opens the course to first- and second-year undergraduates to acquaint them with "what the world of advocacy and policy looks like on college campuses." Having experienced an assault while enrolled in the class, Julia was struck by how, despite all her knowledge about sexual violence and assault, she had not deeply involved herself in the "survivor advocacy space." But the scaffolding that the course provided her enabled her to better understand survivorship and her own identity as a survivor. The course gave her the language and foundation for putting her own experience into broader social and cultural context and to avoid self-blame.

As is true of neoactivists and generations of campus activists in the past (Rhoads 2016, 189), CSVAs' relationships with supportive faculty on their campuses also contributed to their development as activists. Danu, now an alumna of Harvard University, described developing a relationship with a faculty member at the law school who she felt was "really instrumental in helping [her] understand how to better go about [SVA]." Rebecca spoke about how some Princeton faculty supported students at protests by bringing food and coffee, and at UCLA, a faculty member asked Michelle to give a presentation to faculty. Generally, faculty's engagement with student activism was a developmentally positive experience for the CSVAs in our study, often connected to their exposure to faculty's scholarly understanding and theorizing of gender violence.

CAMPUS CULTURE: ALCOHOL, ATHLETICS, AND GREEK ORGANIZATIONS

For decades, researchers have examined student characteristics and campus characteristics that shape student and institutional dispositions toward the proclivity and susceptibility to sexual violence and institutional responses, including men's participation in intercollegiate athletics (Melnick 1992). As the "internal logic" of present-day colleges and universities, discursive masculinity circulates gender norms as the cornerstone of many student cultures (Martínez-Alemán 2014, 116). A campus "drinking culture," whether separate from or integral to athletics and fraternity cultures, has been identified as creating a "high risk" environment for sexual assault, and a dominant component in the ecology of campus sexual assault (Moylan and Javorka 2020, 182).

Rape incidents in which the victim is incapacitated by alcohol (or drugs) are common across campuses in which drinking cultures and other risky social contexts are normative (Warner et al. 2018, 43; Krebs et al. 2016, 93). Though other campus demographics play a role in creating and sustaining risky environments and in supporting campus cultures that further sexual assault and violence, fraternity and athletic campus cultures are most commonly those spaces in the campus ecology of relationships and behavior where sexual assault takes place. Buoyed by a campus drinking culture and reinforced by adherence to masculine norms as they relate to alcohol consumption and sexuality, athletics and fraternities are the epicenters for campus sexual assault.

It is not surprising, then, that CSVAs are also motivated by a desire to counter toxic gender culture and institutional indifference to misogyny commonly found in men's intercollegiate athletics and campus Greek life. Research has consistently shown the relationship between fraternity members' compliance with male gender norms that correlate with the objectification of women (e.g., Seabrook, Ward, and Giaccardi 2018), as well as the promotion of rape culture by institutions when they sanction fraternity parties (Armstrong et al. 2016). Fraternities are a primary contributor to campus cultures that endorse sexual violence toward women (e.g., Corprew and Mitchell 2014; McMahon 2010), and fraternity cultures set peer norms that justify heavy consumption of alcohol correlated with unwanted sex (Seabrook, Ward, and Giaccardi 2018). Heavy drinking at fraternity and athletic team campus parties is a part of many campus cultures that inculcate and support conventional definitions of rape and that are less likely to believe that a sexual assault is rape, also known as "neutralizing" rape (Boyle and Walker 2016, 1403). College athletics peer networks also encourage intoxicated sexual behavior (Locke and Mahalik 2005, 282; Murnen and Kohlman 2007, 150). So it was not surprising that, like other CSVAs, Emily identified Geneseo's student culture as one governed by fraternities, sororities, and athletics, all contributing to a campus peer culture that sanctions rape myth and fraternity party cultural norms. Emily described how fraternity men created PowerPoint presentations of sorority women with whom they had hooked up:

> [T]his guy who was in this one frat . . . He made a presentation of every single [woman] he hooked up with. I was on it. I know like half the girls on it. It was terrible. We didn't know how bad it was. I thought there were like 20 girls on that list, there's like over 100. But no one was talking to each other so we were, like—it was like a huge thing. I mean, there was a drinking game surrounding it. You take a shot if you would hook up with this girl and then rated how good you were in bed, on the PowerPoint.

Kara's observation of Geneseo's culture is consistent with Emily's. SUNY Geneseo is a public liberal arts college of the State University of New York system with a strong fraternity culture. In 2020 Geneseo hosted a rally called "Take Back Geneseo," which effectively spread awareness about the lack of accountability around sexual violence. This event consisted of stories and speeches, where survivors' voices were uplifted and the community at large was encouraged to increase their understanding of sexual assault incidents on campus. Kara remarked that fraternity culture on campus is one in which "taking advantage of [women] who are intoxicated" is not uncommon, and further, that it is sometimes "just so violent." However, as a CSVA, Kara's objective is not to "ban Greek life," knowing that the support for that effort would be nonexistent on a campus dominated by Greek life. Instead, she "worked with them." She noted that "they have been somewhat supportive," though the powerlessness of the college's Inter Greek Life Council makes the work feel pointless.

It's clear to Yashica that the culture of fraternities at Boston University is consistent with sexual assault. She maintained that fraternities are the "one place on campus where [sexual assault] would be most likely to occur," and most specifically at "a frat party, regardless of what fraternity it is."

Sororities on campuses are often complicit in supporting a party culture at fraternity houses. Mixers and parties with alcohol at fraternity houses are often sites where sexual violence and assault occur (Seabrook, McMahon and Conner 2018, 510) and are co-hosted by sororities. At Stanford, Subhadra observed that sororities interact with fraternities, and despite claims that survivors make about assaults at fraternity parties, "the sorority leadership" continues to have parties and mixers with these fraternities.

Like the impact that fraternities have on campus culture and peer relations, men's athletics can also suffuse a campus with "rape-prone" culture (Martin 2016; Sanday 1996), a reality that is especially salient on NCAA Division I campuses (Mordecai 2017). NCAA Division I campuses have significantly higher reports of violence against women compared to the other athletic divisions, and institutions with no athletic programs. Sexual violence at universities with consistently competitive football programs and institutions in certain Division I conferences also show significantly high rates of reported sexual violence (Blanchard, Weinstein, and Rojas 2021, 260; Wiersma-Mosley and Jozkowski 2019, 3–4). It is at these higher-risk campuses in conferences such as the Big 10, Big 12, Ivy League, Pac-12, and SEC that accusations of sexual assault are leveled on members of high-profile football teams (Blanchard, Weinstein, and Rojas 2021, 260; Wiersma-Mosley and Jozkowski 2019, 3–4). CSVAs are very aware of this issue, which certainly does not occur solely among football players. For example, men's collegiate basketball players have also been linked to sexual assault (Huffman 2018; Keene 2021; Keneally and Smith 2019).

The CSVAs most often linked men's football, basketball, baseball, and rugby teams to sexual assault, though baseball was only sometimes mentioned. However, CSVAs focused more on how the culture of sexual assault by men's athletics was maintained and buoyed by coaches who are empowered by their universities to make sure that allegations against their players would "go away" (Kayla, Georgetown University) and that there would be "no repercussions" for sexual assault by players (Alexia, University of Maryland). Kayla believed that much of the power is held and wielded by football and men's basketball coaches, noting "they both hold a lot of power at the University. They're very capable of making things go away." She reasoned that the strength and notoriety of the men's basketball program was an "obvious" impediment to change. Kayla blamed the "culture" of men's athletics on her campus, its prominence and the protection that the team members are afforded, with the inability to enact substantive change.

In sum, CSVAs recognize that the culture and discourse of masculinity prevalent in fraternities and men's intercollegiate athletics on their campuses are insurmountable impediments to change. CSVAs are cognizant of the link between sexual/gender violence and the discursive forms of masculinity that are directly and indirectly supported by institutional agents, policies, and practices. Many scholars have referred to the dominant culture and discourse of masculinity as "toxic masculinity" (Harrington 2021), an analytical concept that characterizes a form of masculinity as pernicious, virulent, and harmful. A gender archetype "toxic masculinity" is used in popular media and academic scholarship to understand the behavior of men—often violent—in public and private settings.

Scholars have raised concerns about the normative nature of "toxic masculinity" as an analytical framework (Harrington 2021) and consequently, its unsuitability to examine nuanced understanding of gender. However, CSVAs describe the culture of men's collegiate athletics (Kayla) and the leniency given aggressors (Alexia), Greek life, and party culture (Kara).

CSVA STRATEGIES

Sexual violence activists on college campuses are like other twenty-first century campus activists (Conner 2020, 3–11). Today's campus activists utilize social media, resist organizing themselves in hierarchies, value fostering a collective vision, and concern themselves with activists' mental health and well-being (Brady 2020, 4–5, Linder et al. 2019a, 92). Like other "digitally aided movements," campus sexual violence activism is "leaderless" in the traditional vein of twentieth-century campus movements and uses social media as only one means to hold their institutions accountable (Gismondi and Osteen 2017, 64). Like other student activists currently on campus, CSVAs organize "without counting on cultural or political revolutions"' but situate their activism and consciousness-raising within important social justice movements (Brady 2020, 4). That said, campus sexual assault activism today is still a relational activity that, like other neoactivism, finds success in changing one person's experience and trauma of sexual violence and in "changing hearts and minds" of campus peers (Conner 2020, 149). Consistent with other campus activists' views of institutional administration (Conner 2020, 186–191), the CSVAs' struggles with administrative resistance reflected their belief that many campus administrators lack cognitive empathy.

ESTABLISHED FORMS OF ACTIVISM

Through traditional activism strategies and present-day technologies, CSVAs engaged in two different and broad forms of "changework" (Marine and Lewis 2020, 225) to enact positive change in the policies and cultures of their colleges and universities. Institutional policy changework includes transforming reporting options, adjudication procedures, and the nature and kinds of resources offered to survivors. Cultural changework includes peer education efforts to shift dominant campus discourses and end toxic traditional student social cultures in institutions (e.g., fraternities, athletics, final clubs). Both forms require CSVAs to build diverse and committed coalitions of other students and student groups (and sometimes faculty and staff).

The CSVAs take a number of actions to enact change by confronting administrators and institutional leaders who hold cultural and structural power, sitting in / occupying powerful administrative spaces, creating and disseminating lists of demands, and leveraging social media to demand accountability from the institution and its officers. Conducting peer education seminars and campaigns and using social media to center survivor narratives are methods used to raise peer consciousness and to validate survivor claims.

Campus sexual violence activism today is still focused on campus face-to-face events and activities, often relying on strategies reminiscent of earlier activist generations. The most dominant form of campus sexual violence activism is the tradition of "visualities" (Arnold et al. 2020, 79). Protests, sit-ins, petitions, signage (both virtual and on-the-ground), meetings with campus administrators, engagements with the campus and local press, op-eds, and various modes of campus disruptions have been the backbone of activism on college campuses and continue to this day. Like many women's movements, these CSVAs seemed to prefer conventional tactics, regardless of the campus targets (Walker et al. 2008). Take Back the Night Marches, sit-ins at the university president's office, and petitions for structural change endure as sexual violence activism strategies. These traditional strategies are performative acts that hold historical and specific contextual meaning. Discursive, whether through images or text, these strategies are a narrative of misogyny that continues to be sustained by campus cultures and institutional structures. Similar to other campus activist groups today (Broadhurst 2014, 12), the CSVAs regularly use traditional face-to-face strategies like sit-ins, marches, and performances to broadcast concerns and grievances.

Among CSVAs, the tradition of protest marches and awareness walks is routine and perceived as unexceptional. Petitions with demands are common, though always focused on improving the experiences of survivors though some structural change. Activists wrote op-eds and alerted the media of their petitions, sit-ins, and marches, all traditional tactics. Eli and other activists at Middlebury College decided to "dress up in varying levels of clothing and hold signs . . . like 'not asking for it,' 'still not asking for it'" (Eli). Activists continue to meet with administrators and campus leaders to present their concerns and their proposals for change. At UMBC, Morgan met with the president who appreciated that their presence as a survivor and nonbinary student represented a set of experiences that had to be shared with the president. The quality and effects of meetings with administrators and university leaders provide another data point for assessing campus sexual assault activism.

As expected, the activist practice of sit-ins common to student activism in the 1960s is still used today by sexual violence activists. Rebecca (Princeton), Anja (Barnard/Columbia), and

Kayla (Georgetown) each described sit-ins that were well planned and orchestrated:

> *[A] lot of planning went into the actual sit in. It was a lot of trying to anticipate, making sure we knew exactly what it was that we wanted from it, making sure we knew exactly what to ask administration for . . . It was like 16 hours of my time a day, you know . . . we only sat in for about a week. So, from Monday to Friday, 9 A.M. to midnight and throughout the course of that hundreds of students sat-in, hundreds and um, I mean people came in and out as they could. Based on schedules, based on their availability. So, like, a lot of times, like early in the morning like 9 A.M., you know, just like that solid five people. . . . But by the time you hit like 4 P.M. you could literally see like. . . . 102 . . . . People couldn't walk through the office anymore. It was like. . . . They had to move the administrators from their offices to a temporary office.*

At Barnard, Anja described a sit-in sponsored by a coalition of student groups for four days at one of the student buildings. Princeton, a private Ivy League research university in New Jersey, has faced student protests on the mistreatment of the sexual assault reporting procedure since 2019. In 2019 an undergraduate at Princeton was fined for damaging campus property after she wrote "Princeton Protects Rapists" on campus walkways to protest the university's handling of her sexual assault case. Rebecca described a common conclusion to student sit-ins at Princeton:

> *[T]he formal sit in concluded after a meeting with President Eisgruber . . . he said that he really sympathized with*

the experiences that he heard in this conversation because the six of us also spoke a bit about how the system had personally impacted us and just also about what we had seen from the protests and what we've seen from the administration. And he reiterated that he felt that the processes that were in place were already fully equipped to handle all of these things and no changes needed to be made. So he was like I sympathize, but I refuse to acknowledge that there's anything wrong, which was sort of a contradiction in itself.

Scholars of campus activism note that conventional activism approaches like sit-ins, marches, and teach-ins seek to cultivate disruption by mobilizing groups of students to interrupt institutional practices (e.g., annual meeting of the board of trustees) and operations (e.g., sustained occupation of administrative offices). Other forms of disruptions like teach-ins are often very disruptive for institutions because they are "more resonant" with the target of the activism, in this case, faculty and administrators (Barnhardt 2014, 45). Activists like Anja are sometimes ambivalent about these disruptions, not feeling sure that the tactic can garner activist demands:

I remember that fall the activists in No Red Tape disrupted the classroom of this executive vice president for student affairs Suzanne Goldberg to protest her treatment of student sexual assault and other [Title IX] issues and I remember being kind of on the fence about that. I didn't understand the lay of the land well enough to understand why that might or might not be a good idea so I sat that one out . . . I think I'm still ambivalent about how effective that particular method is just because of the really strong negative reaction it provokes.

Generally speaking, activists agree that these disruptions can bring attention to their demands, but the CSVAs we interviewed tended to prefer working directly with institutional leadership to change practices and policies, despite the difficulties inherent in that approach. Exceptions include the CSVAs at Boston University, who relied solely on social media as their activist platform and strategy. Instead of working directly with administrators, the BU CSVAs' motivation was to embarrass the institution by amplifying survivor stories on social media. Though the CSVAs interviewed did not include alumni networking or alumni collaboration as an activism strategy, alumni probably were reached through their social media posts and campaigns.

Colleges and universities have embraced social media as a means to communicate and engage with their alumni (Kowalik 2011; Peruta and Helm 2018), so it is reasonable that CSVAs' use of social media may have extended to alumni.

ACTIVISM AND INSTITUTIONAL POLICY TRANSFORMATION

Like all CSVAs, the CSVAs in our study work to promote change in institutional policies that directly impact sexual violence survivors, as well as those practices that undermine existing protections for survivors and students vulnerable to sexual violence. All CSVAs spoke about particular campus policies that were limiting survivor protections and assistance and a lack of administrative commitment to eradicate toxic campus cultures that encouraged sexual violence.

At Barnard College, Anja and other CSVAs focused on the "No Red Tape" campaign that contained detailed demands for improving campus safety, expanding health care for survivors, and improving crisis center accessibility (Taylor 2015). Grounded in a desire to support survivors, Anja's activism at

Barnard was intentionally focused on tangible changes to Barnard's existing policies and practices directed at the larger goals of survivor support and campus cultural change. According to Anja, her campus sexual assault activism at Barnard was securely anchored in the overarching goal to improve support services for survivors, and "No Red Tape" was a movement designed to identify the tangible ways in which the university could make improvements that mattered to survivors. Anja reasoned that it was important to connect survivor experiences with concrete administrative changes. For example:

> *[This means] understanding that lots of survivors do not feel safe at all around the police and understanding that lots of survivors can't afford the $150 on Columbia insurance to go to the emergency room; and that those survivors deserve care and to feel safe just as much as anybody else . . . When we talked to administrators, we'd try to make it really clear that [survivor support] can be realized in multiple forms. One of them could be having Columbia's health center open during more hours, especially during weekends. If not, people go multiple days without necessary care. [Survivor support] could also be realized by having a voucher system or something with a nearby ER room; lots of students can't afford the hundreds [of dollars that the ER room normally charges].*

Anja's activism, like many others who shared their CSVA experiences, was tactical and provided institutions with clear, workable demands. Nadia, for example, outlined the responsibilities of a survivor advocate, an alternative to the reporting through UMBC's Title IX process:

[A survivor advocate] would be on campus so that anyone who is in crisis or dealing with their survivorship could go to this person, get resources, have a centralized location to have their questions answered, figure out if they need to go to a hospital for a rape kit or what next steps they could go through if they didn't want to go to the police or if they didn't want Title IX.

At Howard University, Kayla and other CSVAs also identified structural changes that would improve survivor experience: extending after-hour health services and providing a 24–7 crisis response center. Additionally, CSVAs at Howard identified the need for mental health care services for survivors of sexual assault:

We asked for a trauma specialist . . . they notified us that there was one in the process of being hired. We asked for permanent clinicians, specifically two clinicians, and two queer clinicians and it ended up that. . . . We weren't able to get permanent positions.

In sum, the CSVAs we interviewed continue the traditions of campus sit-ins, marches, confrontations, and meetings with institutional leaders. They collaborate to draft petitions, write op-eds, and alert local and campus media to their activism and its goals. Nonetheless, the CSVAs were pragmatic, seeking to implement structural institutional change through well-directed strategies. Like other social activism, their public expression of criticism levied at institutions is used to provoke reactions from campus administrators as well as motivate or chastise campus peers (Barnhardt 2014, 45). CSVAs' strategies do align with

their campus cultures and consider the institution's vulnerabil-
ities. For example, very aware of how their particular institutions
protect their "brand," CSVAs tactically use local and national
media interviews and reporting strategically to exploit an institution's reputation.

NEW FORMS OF ACTIVISM: SOCIAL MEDIA AND INTERNET TECHNOLOGIES

Social media and twenty-first-century technologies such as file
sharing and storage services like Google Drive have made the
production, dissemination, and consumption of information
fast and straightforward. Among US adults ages 18 through 29,
the use of social media platforms and apps is commonplace.
Platforms such as Facebook, Instagram, Reddit, and Twitter, and
apps like TikTok, SnapChat, and WhatsApp are used regularly
and for a myriad of communication needs (Auxier and Anderson 2021). Online social media are now a ubiquitous aspect of
student culture on campus (Martínez-Alemán and Wartman
2008) and central to all campus activities and operations
(Rowan-Kenyon and Martínez-Alemán 2016). As a tool for sexual violence activism, social media technologies are employed
by CSVAs to raise awareness, gather and post information, and
provide support for their campus activists communities (Linder
et al. 2016, 231). Sexual violence activists use social media to
connect across activist groups and to disseminate appeals for
participation in events. At the University of North Carolina at
Chapel Hill, Andrea noted that social media were used to fuel
the momentum of the Coalition Against Violence. Activists at
UNC, a public research university, have used social media to
spread awareness of sexual assault for at least a decade.

Moreover, CSVAs use social media technologies as a "coun-
terspace to reduce power dynamics present in other spaces"

(Linder et al. 2016, 26). Like other Net Generation activists, sexual violence activists on college campuses recognize the utility of social media like Twitter (Bonilla and Rosa 2015, 7) but understand its utility as unexceptional and conventional. These twenty-first century activists use digital technologies to extend their inter- and intra-campus collaborative reach quite matter-of-factly. These web-based communication technologies are understood by CSVAs as an obvious means to circulate activist information but don't seem to hold any unusual or particularly distinctive activist function. These media are instrumental for carrying out activist work.

The CSVAs interviewed employed online file storage and synchronization services like Google Docs to gather input to draft petitions to administrators. Consistent with their generational disposition, these synchronized shared documents are efficient and effective tools for activism that values and practices collaboration. For example, Rebecca explained her activist group at Princeton would spend hours "in an open conversation where I stood in front of the group of people who had gathered" to read out the demands to be petitioned, and asking for input:

> It was just like a really open conversation where anyone could speak about how they felt like things were missing, how they felt like even wording needed to change, little things like that. And then after this long conversation that was like an open discussion then we were like, okay, there's a shared Google Doc like change what you want. Let's all edit it. Basically, the whole first day into the late night was just editing and changing and representing everyone's opinions.

Messaging applications like Snapchat and mobile group messaging apps like GroupMe are second-nature tools for activists to support each other, strategize, and organize events. Social media networks like Facebook and Twitter serve as information and support kiosks for activists, allies, and survivors. Social media pages are also strategic. For example, Kara intentionally set up a Facebook page, "Take Back Geneseo," reasoning that

> *I planned it for move-in weekend, so I wanted parents to see and I wanted freshmen to see, and I, frankly, was trying to hurt the school and their wallets more than anything else to make a difference.*

At Barnard College, Anja also used social media purposefully:

> *When we write Op Eds I think Facebook is one of the main ways that those get shared. And when we write petitions and such, Facebook is absolutely the way they get shared.*

Campus activist groups use social media advantageously to increase their visibility, skillfully choosing particular sites for particular student populations. Nadia and her group at Maryland found that "Instagram is more successful" than their Facebook page with certain "demographics." She noted that Instagram gave them access to "new or younger students," and that Facebook brought their activism to faculty and staff. Intentionality is the key to campus sexual activists' use of social media. While at UCLA, Michelle knew that in order to use social media effectively, "you have to be really intentional about what you're posting because it can kind of just become another thing someone scrolls past so, like, making sure that it's like useful resources and easy to look at."

BRANDING A MOVEMENT: HASHTAGS AND #METOO

Unique to this generational era of campus sexual violence activism is "hashtag activism." Primarily on Twitter but also circulated on other social media like Facebook, Tumblr, and Instagram, the use of hashtags has enabled activists to share information specific to sexual violence on campus (Linder et al. 2016, 231), announce calls for action on campus, and in ways, democratize their discussion of campus sexual violence. Hashtag activism combines activism's visual presentation of dissent and grievance (e.g., protest marches) with the intensity and emotion of communal response in text (Arnold et al. 2020, 85). Sexual violence hashtag activism maintains the energy of the grievance and injustice salient and active, allowing continuous monitoring of the issue as well as serving to help mobilize future activists (Arnold et al. 2020, 86). As an open-source, interactive communication tool, hashtags can be used to raise awareness of campus incidents, administrative responses to CSVA demands, and to publicize institutional responses to sexual assault cases. Hashtags like #HUForgot (at Howard University), #GeorgetownDoesn'tCare, #JustSaySorry (Tufts University), #AskForBetter (Swarthmore College), and #ourharvardcandobetter muster supporters of sexual violence activists' demands made of colleges and universities, while #MakeVA-CampusesSafe, #MeTooASU (Arizona State University), and #stopvictimstigmatization (Boston College) provide support and community for campus survivors, as well as information about sexual violence and safety. It must be noted that hashtag anti–sexual violence activism is subject to hateful commentary, bullying, and trolling (Lindgren 2019, 422).

To be sure, #MeToo is the paragon for sexual violence hashtag activism. Predating its hashtag address, the "Me Too" crusade was originated by activist Tarana Burke in 2006 on the online social networking site Myspace and intended to communicate to survivors that they are heard and that their experiences are understood. A deliberately public communication, Burke's online posting focused on empathy for and solidarity with survivors of sexual violence and sought to publicly honor and commend survivors. By 2014 hashtag activism that focused on sexual harassment, assault, and survivor support could be readily found on Twitter (e.g., #WhatWereYouWearing, #Survivor Privilege). A little over a decade after Burke's appeal and motivated by the sexual abuse accusations against Hollywood producer Harvey Weinstein in 2017, actress Alyssa Milano used the phrase in a tweet calling on "all women who had been sexually harassed or assaulted" to tweet "Me Too as a status" to "give people a sense of the magnitude of the problem" (Milano 2017). #MeToo was used over 200,000 times the day it was tweeted by Milano, and a year later, approximately 19 million times (Anderson et al. 2018). Today, #MeToo is ubiquitous and global with countless related hashtags (e.g., #TimesUp, #survivor, #sexualassault, #believesur vivors, #womenempowerment, #rapeculture).

For the CSVAs, #MeToo activism (as well as the #MeToo movement) served as a social movement backdrop for their campus sexual violence activism, and as administrators' convenient justification for the perception that there was sexual violence on campus. At SUNY Geneseo, Kara felt that "the Me Too movement definitely influenced the Times Up Geneseo movement." At the University of Maryland, Nadia acknowledged that "Me Too" came to her campus and it ignited a protest that "shook the campus." She was astonished by the power of the crowd that showed up, noting, "I never really have seen that many students out and protesting, and some of them even stormed up to the president's office and kind of had a sit-in where they talked with him."

Most other CSVAs remarked that #MeToo was a cultural moment and social movement that, though pertinent to and useful for their campus work, was more about Hollywood moguls and high-profile powerful men. Rebecca, a 2020 Princeton University graduate, felt that the connection of the #MeToo movement to campus sexual violence activism was ancillary. Kayla at Georgetown held a similar view:

> #MeToo on a national scale started the dialogue more as a society . . . But as far as like our how it informed our work, I wouldn't say that #MeToo necessarily influenced that too much.

The CSVAs all saw the relationship between the #MeToo crusade and their own activism on campus. However, all were very clear that their work to end sexual violence on campus did not originate with sexual assault hashtag activism like #MeToo and was in many ways a separate enterprise, albeit tangentially related. Campus sexual violence activism is concerned with supporting student survivors, dismantling toxic campus cultures that enable sexual violence, and creating new mechanisms for survivor reporting and restorative justice. Viewed as extraneous to their campuses and the campus cultures that promote sexual violence by CSVAs, #MeToo is not a clarion call for their campus activism.

Many of the CSVAs interviewed expressed concern that #MeToo and the #MeToo movement provide campus administrators with an excuse for inaction. Kara recognizes how #MeToo is "problematic," despite its mission and message. She sees how campus administrators see the #MeToo movement as "happening everywhere" so it's "not just [their] problem." Andrea shared this view, noting that as "the movement has become commercialized" and "so mainstream," universities are throwing their hands up, claiming that it is socially endemic and that they can't really do anything about it.

PEER EDUCATION

A surprising number of peer educators responded to our call to talk to us about campus sexual violence activism, suggesting to us that peer education could be understood by current students as a form of activism. At times conducted as bystander intervention education (McMahon 2014, 279–280), peer education programs focused on sexual violence have been found to be an effective means to discuss sexual violence and change student perceptions (Kress et al. 2006, 154; McMahon et al. 2019, 280). Peer education programs and peer discussion groups are viewed as one component of campus sexual assault activism by the activists interviewed. In the tradition of the campus sexual assault activism teach-ins, sexual violence peer education programs are designed to educate students, leveraging the power of students, faculty, and administrators as campus facilitators (Katz and DuBois 2013, 655–656).

Often institutionally sponsored, many of the CSVAs view peer education programs as a means to "teach" their peers about sexual violence and rape myths and as a way to reach survivors. The campus programs aim to dispel the untruths and attitudes that endure about rape victims. A form of victim blaming, these stereotypes and sexist beliefs give license to sexual aggressions against women and condone male sexual aggression against women (Lonsway and Fitzgerald 1994). Some, like Coral at UC

Irvine, are introduced to the campus-based peer education program at first year orientation and begin their activism there:

> *At my [college's] orientation program we had a speaker come in and talk about our Campus Assault Resources and Education office, so our CARE office and she talked about what students could do there, what their programs looked like and they were big on bystander intervention and what it means to support a survivor of sexual assault. It was very brief, I think it was an hour and a half presentation at my orientation but I knew like okay this is where I want to get involved, this is where I need to go. So, I visited the office just to hear more about their services and I found out they were providing free and confidential services to survivors of sexual violence and they put on educational workshops throughout the year about sexual assault and just different activities they had throughout the year. So I spoke with the director and I asked how I could get involved and she let me know that I could apply for a peer education program there because you couldn't just get involved you had to apply and be accepted into a position.*

At the University of California Los Angeles (UCLA), a top-ranking land-grant research university, students have accused the university of inadequately handling issues of sexual harassment and misconduct. Most recently, the university has been criticized for mishandling sexual assault complaints. Students have actively worked to provide support for survivors of sexual assault through events such as Denim Day, Take Back the Night, Baegoals: Defining and Discussing Healthy Relationships, Purple Thursday, and more. Many of these events are supported by UCLA's CARE (Campus Assault Resources and Education program), which focuses on advocacy, healing, and education. At UCLA, Lynnea recalls she leaped into CSVA work through peer education:

> *And then I saw that CARE was recruiting advocates and peer educators, and I thought that that would be such a good way to channel and focus my efforts. And so that I'm not feeling so personally affected by everything that's said to me, because it's so easy for—I think for everyone to just like—especially me, I think—to take things personally when I'm having these discussions and I wanted to actually be an effective advocate. I wanted to be an efficient, effective ally so that I can actually make a difference, rather than getting hurt and just walking away from conversations. That's why I wanted to join it, and I wanted to learn from people who were more experienced in these discussions and conversations than I was.*

She continued by saying that it is the act of peer-to-peer discussion and conversations that "is making a difference." That by "even just engaging in small discussions and encouraging people to learn more about issues of sexual assault and harassment and consent," CSVA concerns are heard. CSVAs Michelle, Coral, and Logan also considered their peer education work as sexual violence activism for these very reasons. At Westminster College, a private, nonprofit, liberal arts college in Salt Lake City, Utah, Logan has engaged other students in conversations around sex-positive activism.

Other CSVAs took their activism to the arts. In 2014 Columbia University student Emma Sulkowicz engaged in performance art activism with her senior thesis, "Mattress

Performance: Carry That Weight" (Davis 2014). Motivated by her experience as a survivor of campus rape and a devastating experience with a failed allegation against the perpetrator, Sulkowicz's performance art inspired Columbia CSA activist group, No Red Tape, to pile 28 mattresses on the doorstep of Lee Bollinger, Columbia's president. Symbolizing the 28 sexual assault complaints in Columbia's Title IX case filed in October 2014, this activist tactic used performance art to confront institutional leadership.

Among CSVAs, poetry, storytelling, and dance were forms of artistic expression used as activism tactics. Alexia said her dance performances "can be very powerful" because they can present survivor stories empathically. CSVA Morgan uses their art to "facilitate the other conversations" in survivor communities "where there's pain from experiences." They see art and poetry "the storytelling of activism" especially for those who do not yet have the language to explain their feelings.

CAMPUS COLLABORATIONS

Consistent with the concept of neoactivism, the CSVAs we interviewed seek out collaborations with a variety of campus groups as part of their activism strategy. Danu speaks of collaboration with College Democrats, Student Labor Action Movement, and Fossil Fuel Digest at Harvard College. At UCLA CSVA Michelle teamed up with the Middle Eastern Students Association. At UMBC Morgan worked with BIPOC groups. Many other CSVAs join forces with their campus LGBTQ+ groups.

Engaging campus fraternities, as Kara did at SUNY Geneseo, is a collaborative tactic that resembles a peer education program. As research has shown, when fraternities engage in sexual violence education, their members change their views in sexual consent and responsibility (Wantland 2008, 64–69). Kara describes her experience with such a collaboration:

> *I reached out to the two most problematic fraternities . . .*
> *Sig Nu's president has actually been very receptive to*
> *change . . . they are trying to reach out and be different, it*
> *does seem, and taking initiatives to take sexual assault*
> *training courses and things like that. They've been recep-*
> *tive to working with me.*

In sum, these CSVAs typified the ecology of twenty-first-century campus activists. Because they recognize the value and worth of genuine inclusion, they build racial and gender diverse coalitions and discern their needs for self-care and mental health. As neoactivists, their actions and analyses of social injustices are critical and intersectional (Conner 2020, 3–9). CSVAs leverage social media to mobilize and effect change, both as a means to educate their campus peers and to make public institutional harms.

CSVAs confirmed that party culture and alcohol play a prominent role in sexual victimization on their campuses. CSVAs believed that unfettered sexual victimization by fraternity members and athletes is often overlooked and discounted by college and university leaders. The effects of their engagement in sexual violence activism on their campuses are many, and yet they persist in their commitment.

In the following chapter, we listen to CSVAs give voice to the weight of sexual violence activism and the effects that both damage and energize them.

Chapter 4

EFFECTS OF ACTIVISM ON ACTIVISTS AND INSTITUTIONS

All activism, no matter the context, has one common direction: change. Yet across human history and myriad social change movements that have defined it, change has often been arduously slow and, at times, imperceptible. Activists' retelling of their time in the trenches of various movements is often typified by the countless hours spent working for change, while change itself is often glacial. As Sullivan and colleagues noted, "progress toward gender equality should always be regarded as a long-term, uneven process" (2018, 264).

This historical trend was certainly reflected in the voices and experiences of CSVAs in this study. In different ways, each spoke forcefully about the ways their work changed the institution and changed their lives as well. In each story, moments of perceptible progress were noted. However, across the stories, we learned that most activists felt unsatisfied with the fruits of their labor. Numerous factors contributed to this, including institutional recalcitrance for support for activists' goals; fluctuations in commitment, strategy, or approach; and the effects of the COVID-19 pandemic. Their dissatisfaction manifested in a constant sense of institutional betrayal (Smith and Freyd 2013, 119) and the recognition that administrators tend to "wait out" their efforts given the inevitably of student graduation cycles. Barnett et al. (2008) described the strategies used by activists as

> rational persuasion, coalition, and pressure. Rational persuasion pertains to the utilization of logical arguments and factual evidence to persuade another that a request is viable and likely to result in the attainment of task objectives; coalition involves seeking the aid or support of others to persuade; and pressure includes the use of demands, threats, or intimidation to gain compliance. (337)

As described in chapter 3, all three strategic approaches were in play across a variety of institutional contexts, all united in the common cause of ending violence. And while notably the CSVAs in our study sensed that institutional change is slow, or altogether elusive, this did not appear to deter their steadfast commitment to the work. Broadly, CSVAs appeared to survive and thrive better when they remained focused on being collaborative and building their numbers and visibility. Visibility provided both a sense of solidarity in the work and a sense that the issue was bigger than themselves. It also provided a counter narrative to the predominant approach espoused by institutions, for whom the primary work of ending violence was focused on apprehending reported perpetrators. CSVAs returned again and again to a critique of the problematic aspects of their college's culture, "beyond the [individual] rapist" (Harris 2019, 5).

Finding connection and coherence with others lent a sense of survivability to the work the CSVAs undertook and meaning beyond whether change actually occurred. Linder and Myers (2017, 190) spoke of the power drawn from collectivity in sexual violence movements and the crucial role of support for their arduous and uncompensated labor. Dismissal of this labor and a general lack of engagement from administrators and faculty discourage CSVAs and forces questions about the meaning of community, safety, and care for students.

From our data, three specific factors shaped CSVAs experiences of change-making: negative experiences such as indifference and institutional betrayal, positive growth and solidarity drawn from unifying around the cause, and the lifelong commitment the work inspired in many.

EFFECTS OF ACTIVIST ENGAGEMENT: INVISIBILITY AND SILENCING

The CSVAs in our study reported almost unanimously that they felt invisible and silent in their primary experience of working with administrators to effect change. This impression was not grounded in an overall sense that their institutional leaders were unconcerned about sexual violence or its effects. Instead, CSVAs perceived that institutional leaders were unconcerned with students' (and especially, CSVAs) concerns and voices about it. Harrison and Mather (2017) recognized this challenge as a fundamental reality of activism: "The source of administrative power lies within the system while activists often find their power by interrupting systems" (120). Interruption was often rewarded with direct circumvention: several participants in the study spoke about institutional leaders deferring authority for their management of the problem to external consultants or to other nonstudent stakeholders (e.g., alumni or advocacy organizations, such as ATIXA, the national organization of Title IX administrators). This choice left student activists, often well versed in federal requirements and having directly relevant campus experience, feeling overlooked for their expertise. As Nadia noted:

> *That was always a point of contention amongst students. There were some who were like, we said all of what these external consultants have said. But it takes these two people that we flew in from California and hired to do this, in order to really pay attention, I guess, to what we'd already been saying.*

CSVAs described spending significant amounts of time studying institutional policies, interpreting them in light of federal, state, and local requirements, and integrating knowledge of student culture to define their appraisal of effectiveness. However, these student-designed interventions, designed and carried out by the very target of institutional policies and programs, were typically not considered relevant to institutional policymaking. The feeling of carrying "the whole weight of the world on their shoulders" (Linder et al. 2019c, 538) was especially acute when marginalization among students was unaccounted for. Often policies were designed to address a generic student experience, when in fact students' experiences were frequently shaped by class, race, and ability status differences as well as numerous other social identities.

These were exacerbated by the realities of the pandemic. Kayla, for example, described the ways that their institution's policy disregarded realities of class difference during the pandemic, in response to students' needing housing to be able to complete academic requirements remotely:

> As soon as the pandemic hit, people needed housing and there were really sizable "asks" from the university to support students in a lot of ways. The university was just like, "Nah," especially when it came to housing, the university was very unforgiving. And was still like dead set on charging students [for housing] even when a lot of them said, you know, right now is not the time. We don't have it. And. . . . housing units. . . . They're already built. . . . you're not losing money, other than electricity and water and whatever it may be. But not every student needed free housing. There were some who obviously needed a lot and it took so much advocacy, it took so much student outrage to get anything done.

CSV activists' belief that they are unheard or ignored often motivated them to develop better, more effective strategies for "upward influence" with institutional leaders (Barnett et al. 2008, 334). Few CSVAs commented that they were deterred by feeling unseen or unheard and simply returned to the drawing board to try again. While many in this study practiced public shaming in an effort to motivate change on their campuses, they were conversant with the realities that public exposure of poor institutional practices could trigger both anxiety and anger from administrators. As Anja noted:

> I feel like I want to figure out how to get them to hear what we are saying would be wonderful because I feel like writing op-eds and stuff, which is basically is like the nuclear option,

like, "Oh, they're tarnishing the university's reputation and professional reputation," it doesn't get them to listen.

CSVAs acted in more intense and visible ways when their sense that they were being ignored was acute. Recalling a student who had expressed fury about being ignored, Rebecca noted graffiti was found on campus in a few different places that said:

"Title IX protects rapists, Princeton protects rapists," things like that. And the university's response to this had been that the girl was fined a large amount of money and her academic status was in question. . . . And it seems like there was no serious thought being put towards what she was trying to say.

This reaction to inaction, reminiscent of the "magic marker terrorists" of Brown University in the 1990s (Schwartz 1990), revealed the ramping up of fury in the face of indifference. These activists used anonymous graffiti, scrawled in visible public places, to warn students about perpetrators and to call attention to the university's indifference to survivors (and other students' safety).

Feeling invisible was connected to their belief that senior administrators, especially, were absent in discussions and demonstrations challenging institutional practice or policy. Their absence signaled to CSVAs that senior-level engagement with the issues was absent and thus that the work was not a priority. Not a single CSVA discussed campus sexual violence policy with a president, and only one CSVA described communicating with a provost. This lack of involvement by high-level institutional leaders was especially notable when compared with other campus activist causes, such as antiracism or disability rights. As Kara, a student at Geneseo remarked:

I haven't really heard much from upper administration and they haven't really talked to me about it much. The president did not come to the march and she had come to—like, she went to Black Lives Matter marches over the summer but she did not come to our march.

Coupled with feeling unheard and unseen, CSVAs frequently commented on the degree to which practices and policies crafted by administrators were frequently perceived as out of touch with student concerns and ideas and did not include activists' suggestions. Instead, CSVAs remarked that administrators frequently advanced a rhetoric of caring about student concerns that rang hollow. Yashica, who led an Instagram-based campaign to amplify survivor stories at Boston University, experienced exasperation with university leaders' rhetoric. She lamented:

I don't want to hear "We are committed." I think we are all very tired of seeing that statement in yet another email saying, "We are committed to protecting our students because we believe that you are an integral part of the BU community." I can give you a quote-by-quote version of every email we've received on that. And I think it's exhausting to read them at this point. I don't know how they keep pumping those emails out. And I understand that the university needs to maintain an image for the public, but what is going to happen to your image when there are thousands of your students coming out with these stories?

EFFECTS OF ACTIVISM: CONCERN FOR MINORITIZED SURVIVORS

Reconciling a message of caring with policies and procedures that reflect a lack of care was especially evident when inequities of access were factored into their reflection. For example, CSVAs were keenly aware of, and deeply impacted by, the disproportionate burden accrued by survivors of minoritized identities, such as those of lesser means. Withholding financial resources, and thereby limiting needed services and programs, was an especially harmful tactic leveraged on activists by administrators. As Anika said,

> We were constantly just fighting, having conversations and trying to get admin on our side, which was not happening and still doesn't. No funding, no nothing.

Financial barriers were frequently cited by CSVAs as a factor in student decision-making; their efforts to address class barriers for survivors were frequently disregarded. For example, at Columbia University, medical services for student survivors were not included in the student insurance plan, requiring a hefty additional copay for students. Anja described the deterrent effect of this policy:

> Understanding that lots of survivors do not feel safe at all around the police and understanding that lots of survivors can't afford the $150 on Columbia insurance to go to the emergency room. And that those survivors deserve care and to feel safe just as much as anybody else, and I feel that Columbia has failed in their institutional responsibility by not providing them with that. That's the really fundamen-

tal part that the administrators don't seem to get and that's what we're pushing for.

Dishearteningly, this is a story as old as time in the context of antiviolence movements. The lack of provision of fair treatment for women with low income and women of color, especially, was pivotal to the emergence of the antirape movement. Further, as discussed in chapter 1, this drove the supporters of Recy Taylor to agitate on her behalf (McGuire 2010, 95). Today, failing to provide inclusive services for student survivors of all income levels has real consequences, as it marks a clear line between who does and does not have the opportunity to pursue criminal charges for an assault.

EFFECTS OF ACTIVISM: DISHEARTENING ENGAGEMENT WITH ADMINISTRATORS

Upon reflection, activists in this study reported experiences with administrators that ranged from annoying to infuriating. For example, activists sometimes bemoaned the lack of the small wins: changes they worked to enact that would cause no real grief or hardship to the institution or its actors and that would be meaningful to students (especially survivors) but that were simply not enacted by university leadership. At Harvard University, activists have criticized the administration for inadequate responses to sexual violence on campus. Student-driven advocacy group Our Harvard Can Do Better continues to work with the Title IX office, among others, to eradicate sexual violence on campus. Like other colleges and universities in Massachusetts, Harvard is required by the Commonwealth of Massachusetts to follow the guidelines set in the Every Voice bill (Bill S. 764 Massachusetts Legislature). But as Danu from Harvard described:

They're thinking about, oh, like we have [the prevention and response office], and we have all these policies but for some people, they think "I have to go to class with my rapist every day" like it's a completely different thing. We're both on different scales and scopes. I think that's where conversations need like, even thinking about how does one report, and the health service doesn't administer rape kits. How can we maybe change that, and if not change that, like, how can we arrange it so that people don't have to get in an Uber alone and be taken, like maybe they can be escorted to Mount Auburn, if necessary? These are things that could be great conversations to have and invite students into, because we're the ones who end up having to go through with those policies.

An additional example was provided by Anja, who spoke of efforts to protect survivors from having to see or be in a class with their perpetrator. Evidence suggests exposure to the perpetrator following a traumatic incident can trigger anxiety and depression and impede educational progress through reduction in GPA (Potter et al. 2018, 497). Several meetings with administrators, and no agreement on a revised policy, left Anja feeling bereft about the possibilities. She, and many other CSVAs, characterized administrators as bureaucrats, saying that "bureaucracy is really made to keep things static and in one place, and the amount of pushback we got for suggesting minor changes is really overwhelmingly frustrating, and I often noted that they don't actually hear what we're saying, they just want to get the meeting over with and get us out of the office."

Machinations of power were operating throughout CSVA interactions with administrators, something to which they were well attuned. Often, sympathetic but disempowered student affairs practitioners would meet students at the front lines of their concerns. However, as Maya stated,

> *these were the people who were very polite, very understanding and very sympathetic but weren't willing to make the changes. So, it was kind of like pushing aside low-level bosses, like it was a video game or something and getting to the faces that were higher up.*

Student affairs practitioners face real challenges when engaging with student activists and often find themselves in two roles: supportive consultant yet also unwittingly representative of the power structure (Markowitt 2009). Danu also spoke of well-meaning, but impotent, administrators, who would equivocate: "I can't say anything officially because my job would be at risk." She noted:

> *People at the Women's Center that I spoke to who are doing great things, like I feel like it would really suck to have their job because I feel like they don't get to do what they want to do, because they have to pander to what the school wants them to do. And so I just, I know that they always like supported what we were doing and didn't feel like we were doing anything wrong, which is really nice.*

Danu also recognized that being too closely allied with institutional officials, even supportive ones, could be problematic. Their allegiance to their employer—understandable, but maddening—made them suspect, even when they expressed support for the students and their cause. Typically, student activists view administrators as either "enemies or antagonists" (Ropers-Huilman et al. 2005, 304). This meant keeping them at arm's length, which often limited their ability to effectively collaborate. Danu named this challenge:

> They [administrators] were really great in some way, but I don't really wish they were more involved because they are part of the institution and so it raises the question of like . . . should they really be part of the institution? I feel like maybe there's room for like a third-party thing because it doesn't feel like they can really do what they want to be doing.

In the cases where senior administrators were viewed as making space for conversations with students, CSVAs believed that they did so only to placate activists and reinforce the policies currently in place.

While most administrators were perceived to be indifferent or hostile to CSVA concerns, several students were quick to name administrators—primarily entry- and mid-level student affairs administrators—who were deeply aligned with their goals and efforts. Speaking of the support received from a key advisor who directed her college's women's center, Nadia expressed:

> When we founded [survivor student group] We Believe You, [the advisor] came on as the advisor for the group. All student groups need an advisor, which can be a faculty or staff member. And she was really excited with the group and the potential with having a survivor discussion group . . . she was really supportive and the Women's Center, not only did we have meetings there, but they provided us with resources and connected us with the people that could have potentially changed things that we had issues with. You know, the Women's Center had already been doing this work and they still are. They go above and beyond what

they are told to do and paid to do. But they were very help-
ful and frankly, instrumental in getting us to where we are
now. They have been almost as deeply involved in Retriever
Courage as we have. The only difference being that we're
students using our free time to do it. But they are employ-
ees who are using their free time to do it. So, it's been great
having them and we certainly rely on them a lot.

Early career administrators, who may have their own histories of agitation as students, often must work to carefully develop
and sustain boundaries with the students they work with. Dis-
cerning appropriate limits to involvement in their work, versus
support of their work, can be a career-long dance for those who
act as "tempered radicals" in the university (Kezar 2010, 457).
Navigating administrative power structures became second nature to many activists in our study, and while time intensive, revealed possibilities for alliance that were previously occluded
by the assumption that "all faculty/administrators are hostile to
our cause." As Subhadra described, the shades of grey inherent
among leaders within these structures enabled some real progress to happen:

One thing that has been super helpful is finding allies with
power within the structures. Whether it's professors like the
one that ran the class and stuff. Tenured professors have a
little more power to say things and push the envelope a little
bit, than we do as students and things like that. Adminis-
trators working within prevention spaces and stuff like that
has been super helpful to find in our activism.

CSVAs spent a great deal of time deliberating whether administrators were obstacles or potential allies, weighing the odds

of meaningful collaboration versus hurtful antagonism. The appraisal was rarely black or white, but instead, the specter of "the administration" hung out in a more liminal, and less predictable, grey zone, as Subhadra described:

> *I think there are some administrators that in the face of these new Title IX changes, have actually become more supportive to students. But these are not the administrators I feel that have the most power. I think they are—they are definitely in positions of power and can affect some change, but I think the ultimate decision makers have not—are still pretty hostile to students, even if they are not openly to your face.*

Coping with intractable policies, constantly having to negotiate and develop new strategies, and building relationships with more and more administrators in the service of change typified the narratives of the CSVAs in our study. As we listened to their stories of repeated persistence in the face of either indifference or hostility, it became clear that these experiences were impactful to various degrees. CSVAs in this study were rarely dissuaded from their cause by administrative intractability, yet most spoke ardently of the difficulty of maintaining mental and physical well-being in the face of such antagonistic treatment. Across their stories, three common reactions to these realities— coping with institutional betrayal, coping with exhaustion and vulnerability, and dealing with feelings of inadequacy—surfaced repeatedly in their words.

NEGATIVE IMPACT OF ACTIVISM: INSTITUTIONAL BETRAYAL

Virtually all CSVAs in this study shared stories that reflected what Smith and Freyd (2014) named as institutional betrayal.

Institutional betrayal was a frequent experience for CSVAs and is defined as "trusted and powerful institutions (schools, churches, military, government) acting in ways that visit harm upon those dependent on them for safety and well-being" (Smith and Freyd 2014, 575). This betrayal took several forms but was commonly described as a sense of being villainized and held responsible for causing disruption to an otherwise placid and congenial community. Activist Andrea Pino, prominently featured in *The Hunting Ground* documentary and who held the University of North Carolina accountable in 2013 for violating Title IX, described it as follows:

> *This happens all the time: They just treat you like a pariah, as a villain when, here's the thing right like I would literally come to these meetings with my ideas, I would come with the law, I would highlight the dear colleague letter, and say, "This is what we're not doing, here's what we could be doing instead." Like I remember I came with a little pie chart, "this is the work that people are already doing, just connect the departments and make life easier for students". . . . it wasn't that hard, but there was this inability to see me as a partner in this work . . . [they assumed] "She's gonna sue," and I'm like you know what? I guess I am. And really it wasn't even just that then they started retaliating. They started putting me on probation on my RA job. They started making my life a living hell when I simply was just trying to help them.*

Many study participants experienced institutional betrayal, but for some students, it was simply reinforcing what they already knew: institutions will demand your love but will not love you back. Students of color, LGBTQ+ students, and students with low income were more conscious of this reality, given past experiences with marginality that were simply reiterated in activist spaces. Jennifer Gómez (2021) has written persuasively about the specific experience of compounded marginality vis-à-vis sexual violence and the reality of experiencing not only institutional but also intracultural betrayal. Gomez observed, "without instantiations of inequality like racism, cultural betrayal itself would not exist, as the betrayal is theorized to stem from the violation of (intra)cultural trust that is developed within-group to guard against such inequality" (101). Racism's perniciousness meant that activists of color in this study had little hope they would be treated fairly by their institutions, as reflected in Morgan's words:

> *Institutions have been letting me down my whole life, not just as a survivor but as a Black nonbinary person that's just how institutions work for me. I come in and I know I'm not going to be addressed; and it's unfortunate but that's just how my entire life has been. So I go in thinking I'm gonna be let down, which isn't okay but that's more of a, that's kind of how I have to operate to survive and not be so wounded throughout my entire life. I went into college knowing that there will be times that I was going to be hurt because of who I am and the identities that I hold because that's just the way the world spins.*

Frequently, we found ourselves impressed (and disheartened) by the degree to which students understood the subtext of administrators' actions: toleration without substantive desire to enact change. Julia, a former student activist at Stanford, spoke of this in especially clear ways, echoing the experiences Chanel Miller described. In the memoir *Know My Name,* Miller wrote about being raped by a student athlete at Stanford and working to hold him accountable through both the university and the criminal justice system (2019). Her activism in turn inspired campus activists to create a memorial garden in her honor, as Julia described:

> *The tricky part, of course, is getting them to take your advocacy and turn it into policy, which has been an uphill battle there. I certainly got a sense of that from Chanel's book as well, that there's been—and the whole thing with the garden and at every turn, anyone who follows what's going on at Stanford sees what looks like a group of pretty recalcitrant administrators and kind of just constantly interfacing with students, but yet, not really doing the right thing.*

NEGATIVE IMPACT OF ACTIVISM: EXHAUSTION AND VULNERABILITY

Exhaustion was a very real phenomenon in the stories we heard. CSVAs spoke of the strain of adding activism to already full schedules as students, athletes, organizational leaders, and workers, all while also aiming to have a robust and rewarding social life. In *The Body Keeps the Score* (2014), Bessel van der Kolk discussed the ways that trauma literally reorganizes the brain's functioning pathways, noting that "trauma is not just an event that took place sometime in the past; it is also the imprint left on mind, brain, and body" (21). Because many of our activists were also survivors, we understood that the bone-weariness of "the good fight" permeated their souls as well as their bodies.

Emily's commitment to activism also relegated many of her other activities to the back seat, and she was left coping with fatigue and a sense of déjà vu:

Yeah, we're going to talk about [sexual violence]. We'll have meetings about it. We're going to do this thing, but it all just poof, it goes away, and then I have four tests in two weeks and then it's like three weeks later and then you don't know what just happened. So it was like that cycle over and over and over again and as you go up, you know, in years, things get harder, for the most part, so then you have less time to be pushing at the administration for change. So I feel like they were just yessing us until we got busy and went away.

Balancing the demands of activism with other facets of college life often entailed making difficult choices, which reverberated in students' personal lives. Eli's status as a student was in peril during a particularly active semester of organizing, a situation that left them vulnerable to challenges for their mental and physical health, shifting their social circles in turn:

Academically, I was stressed. I was really overwhelmed and hadn't yet figured out how to balance anything, especially organizing, so just generally super stressed. I did pretty well academically but I also had five incompletes in my final semester, so it wasn't the best. And yeah, socially I went through a lot of different groups and I think a very big piece of that is, it's a small campus there aren't a lot of people so whenever you do something everybody knows it. So I would say I isolated myself from a pretty big chunk of campus pretty early on like limited/changed over time social experience.

Laura Finley (2013), a sociologist at Barry University, echoed this most poignantly when she wrote: "Raging because I am tired, oh so tired, of my activism being repressed or limited by bureaucratic minutia and ridiculous protocol. I am even more upset at the ways bureaucracy stifles my students who, because they are informed and outraged, want to act and are told they can't, or can only under certain conditions."

CSVAs also spoke of the realities of navigating institutional requirements and policies to enact their activist efforts, a situation that frustrated Emily:

> *I would spend one day a week just doing paperwork for the Women's Action Coalition just to get an event because I was the event planner for three years, just to get a permit to walk around the campus. Just to get access to one extra security guard for Take Back the Night. It would be like I'm pulling teeth for these people. And then, that's also a barrier. I never really thought about this, but that's a barrier for every other activist organization that could happen. . . . The moment that you figure out Geneseo, you don't because a secretary will tell you something different. Organizing events meant always giving entire days of my life away.*

Burnout was a common feature of their narratives and was amplified when students felt their work was crossing over into other aspects of their lives. Unsurprisingly, numerous participants gravitate toward academic subjects that reflected their interests, a symbiosis that was not always positive. As Alexia remarked:

> *I feel like because my classes were about activism and social justice and a lot of unlearning and seeing things for what they are—in my class I was hearing this and in my other spaces—and I worked at the Women's Center as well. So at a point, at my work it was like this and then when I was working on my projects, I was thinking a lot about issues*

*and trauma. . . . it circles around in your head so much
that it's hard to kind of click it off when you need to. When
you're out of that. So I think I learned that the hard way.
I just was really burned out.*

Resource limitations faced activists in ways similar to survivors seeking services. Many activists in this study spoke of the
sheer exhaustion of leveraging time for activism when their very
existence at the institution was in question. Anika, for example, stated:

*I think as someone who faced a lot of rent issues during my
time at UCI, and how much I did not get support from
the campus, and had my friends, who are also struggling
with rent and support, had to help me out or having to ask
my parents, who are already struggling to pay rent in L.A.,
to help me. Because my job also doesn't pay me enough to
pay rent. What does that say about your support services?
Like, where are your—what is the point of having a student services support center, or whatever they called it, and
the only support is: how do you study during finals? you're
not really supporting students. I think they need to reeval-
uate what they think support is.*

The deep care and emotional investment activists placed on
the work meant that the stakes were high for them. Community organizing required significant outlay of personal energy
and time. In addition to frustrations with institutional leader
disengagement, their efforts were often fraught with vulnerability if the activists were confronted with apathy or hostility
from peers, as Kara described:

I will say that by the time we got to the [take back the night] march I was, like, I just need this to be over . . . that horrible feeling when you're the leader and you just want it over with, but I was so stressed for weeks. Some people were telling me that frats were going to confront us in the streets, someone was saying they weren't. Those types of worries on you constantly are very difficult, especially when you're trying to do so much else. And it is really frustrating if the school doesn't step forward and help me. It's upsetting to me with the diversity coordinators and things like that, they don't see this as valuable enough to help. They didn't promote this march, where other marches they sent emails about it and stuff and I will say I didn't ask them to. I wanted to see if they'd pick it up on their own. I needed to see that for myself, to see if they were going to take a step to get involved because, frankly, if they weren't going to get involved by themselves, I wasn't going to drag them into getting involved with me because the issue is them.

CSVAs in our study also reported feeling fearful for their safety and others', as a result of perceiving that protecting perpetrators was a higher priority for the institution than ending sexual violence. Activist vulnerability is common. For example, sexual violence activists at University of Massachusetts–Amherst, for example, have been harassed online and in person by fraternity members (Krantz and Carlin 2021, A16). Nadia was spurred to activism by witnessing this reality and coping with its effects throughout her college career:

My best friend was assaulted on campus, and I was there with her on the evening it happened, and I was there through

*the whole Title IX process. I was the main witness and we
were on the same team together. The perpetrator was also
on the team with us. It was a very delicate situation. We
were freshmen, not really sure about Title IX too much. We
kind of knew what it was, we'd heard about it and never
thought obviously we would need it. But we went through
the Title IX process and at the beginning of our sophomore
year, we were told that there wasn't enough evidence to
find guilt. And that they weren't going to do anything. He
was allowed to continue his education and graduate with
no problem.*

CSVAs in this study often represented a myriad of identities and were conversant with the disproportionate burden
placed on marginalized students to represent social change in
their lives and activism: many also identified as doubly (or more)
marginalized and lamented the extra burden this meant for them
and their peers. Nadia, for example, observed:

*These issues are affecting people of color, women of color, and
LGBTQIA individuals the most and we want to work with
them and we need to work with them. If there is just barrier after barrier to do this work, they are not going to be
there and they can't be faulted for that. But it's also on the
job of the administrators to make it more accessible to them
so they can do the work.*

Activists noted the costs for themselves and others, and in
so doing, signaled the possible futility of the work. As Eli remarked, "I think people are doing a lot of good stuff, it's just
like, I worry sometimes and it's at the cost of the self in a way
that's not really that great."

NEGATIVE IMPACT OF ACTIVISM: FEELINGS OF INEFFICACY

Perhaps the most impactful negative outcome of participating in activism is the sense that the activism is ineffectual and thus that students' work is extrinsically unrewarding. Frequently, when asked what participants saw as the outcomes of their labor and care, many paused and offered some variation of "I'm not really sure" or "I don't think there are any." Emily, for example, who was involved in activism during her entire college career, noted the Sisyphean nature of activist work:

> It sucks to see like we're all—we were freshmen, we've told these stories, now we're seniors and we're still hurt, and there's no evolution, there's no change. We've done nothing, and now we're here. And then we just go home. It just was so disheartening to see that no one has made any progress in themselves, and also now there's even more girls talking about it. So it's like what are we doing? Because obviously what we're doing isn't working.

The intensity of investment in working for concrete change was difficult to swallow when activists reflected on how to reconcile it with actual change. Peers allied in the work did make a difference, but it was often mediated by the feeling that progress was elusive. As Morgan lamented:

> I'm so lucky I had the support that I had, but even with that, the experience was just going going going and then hitting that final plateau; and then the experience of looking up and realizing that things have changed but there's been like no real concrete change that I can say; like the

next person that comes in this happened to will have it bet-
ter because again just students vs the entire institution. I
think in all of my activist work I kind of woke up at one
point and realized like, what concrete change has happened
and it was like a crash.

POSITIVE OUTCOMES OF ACTIVISM: MEANINGFUL PEER RELATIONSHIPS

While challenges were abundant for those who engage in regu-
lar, sustained activism related to ending sexual violence, CSVAs
in this study also experienced a number of positive outcomes.
These included a sense of deepened friendship and solidarity
with others, growth in self-confidence from exercising one's convictions, and finding meaning and purpose in the work itself
separate from outcomes.

Friendship is often wrought through facing adversity alongside others, and this was certainly true for the activists in this
study. Many reported that the most meaningful outcome of the
work they did was the strength and depth of the friendships
formed in solidarity with other activist peers. Neoactivists (Conner 2020, 93) referred to this feature as the "emotional support
aspect" of the work; Marine and Trebisacci (2018) noted that
such solidarity procured a stronger sense of commitment to the
cause. The emotional labor performed by student activists often involved creation of space for survivor stories and solidarity
around them. For those who identified as survivors, this connection was powerfully healing. Regarding her time spent
organizing at Princeton, Rebecca captured this reality, stating,
"It felt like we were all like supporting each other, and people
break down so often, and in those moments everyone was sort

of coalescing around that person like providing them with what they needed."

Depth of connection for activists in this study was often initiated by shared involvement in activism but frequently surpassed simply "doing the work" together. Lewis and Marine (2015) discussed the ways that feminist activists derived a sense of connection that transcended the work. Activists also held one another lovingly accountable for self-care, supporting each other in removing themselves from the work as needed. As Julia, an activist from Stanford, noted:

> *I definitely have found such a strong community that—I mean, these are some of my closest friends even outside of organizing, when we're not talking about anything. And I think that really keeps me going as well. And they are very good—one, about pushing each other to do work, but also pushing each other to tap out for a little bit, because they recognize that you need to step back. . . . to feel uncomfortable, to say I need to take a step back.*

Supporting friends personally affected by sexual violence or drawing on their own suffering to fuel these connections often led to engagement in activism for change. Nadia spoke about her experience offering support to her survivor roommate and how this experience shaped both their friendship and their work together, saying:

> *Just thinking back to when me and my friends started We Believe You, it was how can I help stop someone from feeling how I'm feeling right now. . . . I was able to hold my friend's hand through her Title IX case and I was able to*

help her work through things, and she helped me, because it was traumatic as a survivor to be that witness to someone else's trauma, that we helped each other and we were able to create We Believe You. And it always has been, how can somebody else avoid this? Through preventative work, through new resources—my reward is no student feeling like they have nowhere to go.

Students conducting anti-gun-violence activism under the hashtag #NeverAgain experienced deep connection to one another, which generated more and better activism and ideas, and fueled by their obsessive desire for change. The togetherness they experienced magnified and multiplied their work; it was this that made it special and lasting. Jenny Odell describes this effect as "the communal 'I-Thou' relationship in the 'space of appearance'" (2019, 177). Odell describes this space as a shared space of empowerment in which all are seen, heard, and accounted for (2019, 177).

In some cases, CSVAs in this study had little to no personal connection to the survivors whose voices they amplified, since their efforts were limited to the use of social media to raise awareness. Despite the absence of personal connection, the satisfaction of amplifying survivor voices was genuinely motivating to Boston University students who identified as CSVAs. This counters the assertion that social media is a space where relationships are abstract (Odell 2019, 177) but affirms how shared commitments to end sexual violence on campus can make virtual relationships tangible. Yashica, who grew up without meaningful support for using her voice for social change, explained how even removed and distanced connection fueled her work:

When people say, this account makes me feel heard, it makes me feel seen, it makes me feel believed, that means the world to me because of my cultural background. I grew up in an environment where women aren't heard. Where we don't have voices. And again, I think that's a huge part of my cultural background, and I should mention that. Because that's a huge part of why I am the way I am. Why I'm doing this. Just a lot of "whys" are answered by my cultural background. So I think the most rewarding part is just when people tell me that it's helping, in any way. Even if it's only helping for 0.01 percent in your healing process. In your awareness. In anything. If it's helping, that is the most rewarding part. I think the minute it just helps one person, and I know that's super cheesy, I bet you can find that quote anywhere else, but it is true. At the end of the day, when you help one person, you have this warm, light, fuzzy feeling inside of you. I think that's the best part.

The gratification of being a trusted receptacle for survivor stories was a powerful motivator for CSVAs in this study. As noted earlier in the book, many of the activists in our study were survivors themselves; many others were motivated in the work by deep love for a survivor friend or family member. Lynnea named this factor when she spoke of the vulnerability inherent in calling oneself a survivor:

I think for me, the most rewarding part of this experience is just when people come forward and want to share their experiences with you, because you've kind of given them that security and made them understand that you are there to support them. Because I think that that's so hard to do. No matter who you're talking to, it's hard to open up about experiences like this.

Building solidarity among activists, feeling less alone, and drawing on that togetherness to quell imposter syndrome tendencies was a key aspect of the work for many activists in our study. In fact, when students in our study described being alone, or one of two or fewer working to prevent sexual violence, they often described losing steam and losing confidence. Community yielded a stronger sense of the value or the work and the obligation to continue. Alexia aptly described this accountability factor in her own work:

I think just a personal reward of mine would be bringing my community together. That was really satisfying to me. And seeing that if one person got something really powerful from it, that's what I need. . . . . That's what I wanted to bring and offer to the table. So any challenges or obstacles up to that point, I feel like I'm okay. I helped someone. And seeing the people also support me and support this vision that's kind of hard to advocate for if it hasn't really been done before. You kind of just feel like, who am I to be doing this? Should I be doing this? And having people show up and really believing in you. That's very satisfying. It helps me keep going.

Despite the nearly constant stream of personal connections wrought by shared concern for sending sexual violence, relationships in activist communities were not always problem free. Kayla spoke of a dynamic within the Black survivor–centered group she was part of, in which students shared names of perpetrators, which then became contested. She observed:

Especially because like we dropped [accused students names] into the Hoya Blacks group chat. And for a lot of people, their first instinct was, "We have to protect these people, these people who are being accused wrongfully," or whatever it may be. Right, so it didn't progress very far outside of the Black community until months after.

Naming the potential dysfunction in activist groups was not an admission of their brokenness, but merely an indicator of the complexities of human relationship that infuse many social movements (Parker and Hackett 2012). Maya described this when she named the realities of the dynamic within her survivor-activist group at Georgetown:

I think a lot of activists are also familiar with, you know, dealing with egos . . . but some people did not have the right reasons for joining. Again, it was to, you know, have their face be in the right place but they weren't doing any of the work. And so that led to a lot of accusations of being too exclusive. . . . And so then we would get accusations of, "Well aren't you trying to make the campus, like, you know, a better place for everyone? Like, why aren't you letting these people say their apologies and make their amends?". . . . It was difficult to stay focused on the work while also having to deal with [this]. And so we had to put a lot of emotional labor into it that I don't think we were quite ready for. But I mean, we got through it and we learned but I wish we had gotten a heads up that emotions were going to get that high . . . We had to learn how to be mediators, activists, therapists to an extent and that's hard to do on top of course work.

POSITIVE IMPACT OF ACTIVISM: PREPARATION FOR ACTIVISM AFTER COLLEGE

As a century of research on college outcomes attests, higher education is often an experimental ground for developing and solidifying one's postcollege commitments and avocations, and this was certainly also true of the activists in this study. Several activists, including Danu, hailed the very concrete organizational skills derived from the work. As she noted, "I learned how to effectively organize things, how to have conversations with the people involved in the school like administrators, talking to the people at the title IX [office], things like that."

For those who graduated, morphing their activist commitments into a different form of investment was an important step. For some, like Alexia, their postcollege careers reflect the commitment they honed in college to antiviolence activism. Alexia currently works for an organization that develops and implements shelter-based services for survivors of trafficking and violence.

Eli, intending to enroll in law school and planning to continue their advocacy, described the unintentional forging of their future vocation:

> It's funny, I didn't realize until I graduated that "organizer" was a job. That's what I had been doing. It was actually pretty funny. I definitely think I was drawn to that type of work before I even realized it was something you could do. As a job, it's different than what you can do as a non-affiliated, not-employed person.

Coral has continued her work on sexual violence activism in a very direct way, as a counselor at a rape crisis center, which will also inform her future as an attorney. She noted the abundance of pathways that could lead directly to a career in what she values most:

> *I supervise the 24-hour sexual assault hotline and START response. So I go to the hospital, accompany survivors there, and I supervise the volunteers and train them. So I'm getting really good experience here. I'm looking at applying to law school right now. I want to focus on violence prevention, specifically. And there aren't a whole lot of programs— at least through my research—that are set up for that specifically. So I'm looking at JD programs, because I would like to work at some upper management levels for a nonprofit—maybe a rape crisis center, but also I'm looking at Masters of Public Administration, Public Policy, Master of Public Health—programs like that, because I want to stay centered in this work. I'm looking at what is the best way to do that? And what's the best way to set myself up for success?*

Wisely, activists in this study honored their instincts regarding the limits of engaging in lifelong commitments to ending sexual violence—particularly those who were survivors. Kayla claimed their desire to engage in the work in an ongoing way but set limits on its connection to sexual violence, stating:

> *I want to be an organizer, I think. This is definitely what I want to do with my life. I mean, right now I'm also working with the collective action for safe spaces off campus. I don't want to be organizing around sexual assault long term because of how ultimately draining it is for me personally. . . . But I want to make sure that I'm always*

*organizing and always advocating for the most margin-
alized people in our society . . . I want to do tenant
organizing, worker organizing. I want to support poor
Black and brown people, and you know do what I can to
make this country a little bit better and a little more
inclusive.*

ACTIVISTS' STRATEGIES FOR CHANGE

In addition to reconfiguring the relationship between and
among activists and other campus leaders, strategies for concrete
change abounded in the narratives of the activists centered in
this story. Here, we share some of the most persuasive and salient ideas that activists presented regarding necessary changework in the service of ending sexual violence.

Perhaps most urgently, student activists in our study named
the need for identifying, and adopting, more effective prevention approaches throughout campus communities, to reduce the
need for response services and adjudication policies in the first
place. Currently used prevention technologies, such as the
"canned virtual programs" whose widespread use on college
campuses now functions as most colleges' only form of prevention work, have yielded little demonstrable outcomes. Bystander
intervention, offering a modest amount of evidence supporting
its use, is another frequently used technology of prevention on
many campuses (Kettrey and Marx 2019, 214–216). And yet
activists' perception, by and large, is that on their campuses,
many students simply do not understand what sexual violence
is, what causes it, or what their institutions' stances against it
consist of. To that end, deeper, more comprehensive, and more
sustained education is needed. As Eli noted:

I also think as an institution, it would be great if Middlebury was way more proactive about providing resources for people to know what sexual violence is. It's not just literally a three-hour course at the beginning of the year and then programs that you can opt in or opt out of . . . the kind of education [telling] what sexual violence is, what intimate partner violence is. What that looks like and that is mandatory for students to do. And that lasts longer than just one day. I think it would be a big thing that they could do.

Peer educators and activists also lamented the ways that the labor of activism is rarely recognized and almost never compensated. This prevents a more diverse group of students from taking part in it, as some will be always hampered by the need to do more remunerative forms of work. To this end, Nadia described an idea she had:

One of my suggestions that I'm making at UMBC is a stipend or something. It doesn't have to be large, but you need to increase student retention and belonging in this work. And if that's a $100 stipend a semester or something, cough it up. I mean, I did the work for free and I still am. I don't want to do it for free, obviously.

Activists spoke persuasively about the necessity of leaders orienting themselves first and foremost to understanding, a practice that comes always and only through careful, attentive listening. The effect of careful listening is that it conveys not only that the speaker's voice matters, but that the speaker's personhood matters. Nadia spoke to this quality and practice ardently:

I think firstly, don't listen to respond, just listen to listen. If a student is telling you that something happened to them, believe that it happened and then hear whatever else they have to say about their experience. . . . Whatever it is, listen to listen. You have to start there, otherwise it's always: I'm just responding to you as a student because I'm here in this job above you and you are a student. What do you know?

Kayla spoke to the paradox of experience: that with more time in a job, and with elevated status and position, decision-makers become separated from the day-to-day experiences of student lives and the rich solution spaces their experiences provide them. Kayla notes the perception is that "Administrators are so detached, they are so far up that it's really difficult for them to actually understand the student experience to actually understand what actions there are, that would be helpful for [students]." To counter this, Kayla's advice was to remember and work to stay grounded in the students' experience. She explained:

So, a lot of times they [administrators] give us solutions, but they're not solutions that we would have chosen. They're not solutions that we find helpful. And ultimately, we are the people that they're supposed to be serving and are supposed to be trying to make this campus better, so I think it's ultimately really about prioritizing students and input and understanding that like students know, best to a degree about like exactly what direction we want to move in as a university exactly what we want to see represented exactly what resources we need. Only students can tell you that. *But a lot of administrators have the idea that because they've been in their position so long, they know more. [emphasis added]*

Activists often lamented that the detachedness that administrators and faculty experience when listening to students is compounded by an inability to step out of their own frame of reference. And yet, this is exactly what is needed when coming together to determine shared concerns and forge new ground together. Yashica observed:

> *If someone is truly committed, they will do their best to understand it, regardless of how old they are. And although they will never be able to understand it, just like I won't, because I'm not a survivor, we can still try our best. You can still put in an effort. That's all we're asking. We're not saying, you know, understand this and you need to get every single detail of it. We're just saying we want to see real effort.*

Activists bring knowledge born of experience when crafting solution spaces to end violence, and yet rarely do they see their knowledge validated as data. Alexia proposed an alternative solution that recognizes and validates the work done by activists:

> *Our school has this big research day and through that, they offer a lot of scholarships to do that research. A lot of people apply for those grants. It's like a thousand or $1500 to do a project or research of some sort. I wonder if they could also offer that to a small group of activists on campus, and it could be viewed as activist research.*

Essential to bridging the chasm between activists and institutional administrators is remembering that students' desire to do activist work is born of necessity, as Julia described:

> *There is a reason that we more often than not disagree, which is part of the reason I have to be there in these meetings, if that makes sense. So just recognizing that students are not there to—just for the sake of making administrator's lives hard—we're there to advocate for ourselves and for our peers, and because it's needed.*

Julia continued by suggesting that administrators must also be prepared to do the groundwork and examine research and other sources of science-based intervention, to bring meaningful solution spaces forward:

> *It's not our job to have all of the answers, and what I consider my job is to seek out and elevate student perspectives on what's not working. Often, the response that we get when we bring up a concern to administrators, is like, "So what should we do instead?" Like, if you can't suggest a better alternative, we're not going to change. I would love to emphasize that it's not my job to know the legal constraints or the case law—I don't know what I don't know. All I know is I've heard this concern from students, and you are administrators, and it's your job to fix it. . . . . to not recognize the fact that we have legitimacy and authority in what we can speak to, which is the student experience. That's what we have to offer. Not to correct us on that, but also not to expect that we can really have expertise in anything more than that.*

SUMMARY AND CONCLUSION

As reported by the activists in our study, the work they did was highly meaningful but often carried a significant emotional and personal cost. The impact on the institutions where these activists conducted changework was admittedly modest and was constantly mediated by experiences of marginality, indifference, and sometimes, hostility to the work. CSVAs drew significant sustenance from one another and from amplifying voices of survivors; they formed deep relationships with one another, from a sense of community and solidarity. Their work then took on greater meaning and became more sustainable. Many continue to do the work professionally or as an extracurricular activity. The cost was high; the rewards surpassed it. But real change was elusive.

Finally, as the CSVAs reported, the work was motivated primarily from an urgent and compelling desire to continue until it became obsolete. As Anja eloquently said,

> *I think part of it is that I'm not sure I could not do it. It's really important, I feel viscerally that it's important and that's really important to me as what has been driving me. I think also, there's something about writing an op-ed or a petition and seeing it be shared and seeing people become aware of an issue. . . . that* does *feel like having an impact.*

Chapter 5

POWER, VOICE, AND STRATEGY

When we began this project, our aim was to center the voices, concerns, and experiences of campus sexual violence activists, anticipating that they would offer ways to recalibrate gender discourses and the discursive nature of institutional power that shapes policy and practice around sexual violence on college campuses. Currently these discourses are dominated by a focus on compliance with the federal government and its designated technology of interruption for violence, Title IX (Marine and Nicolazzo 2017, 5009). By listening to CSVAs, we can see the merits of a more effective approach to ending gender-based violence on college campuses that relies on institutional courage (Center for Institutional Courage, n.d.) and power-sharing. It replaces the short-term reward of compliance with the more arduous but longer-lasting commitment to cultural change on our campuses. It brings the strengths of the various constituencies into sharp relief, drawing on their most salient attributes to effect change. It rejects the cynicism of "us/them" oppositional thinking, in favor of "we-us" connective subjectivity. But to propose a different way of being, we must first engage a different way of thinking about three specific stress points inherent in sexual violence-related changework on college campuses: power, voice, and strategy (Marine and Lewis 2020).

INSTITUTIONAL POWER AND ACTIVISM

A prevailing theme in the narratives of activists in this study was awareness of (and frustration with) the role that formal power plays in the development of institutional policy and practice, a theme that extended beyond simplistic notions of the (dis)empowered student-facing powerful administrators. As Danu reflected about the Title IX administrators at her university,

> it always feels like they're trying to help us as much as they can, but their superiors are the administrators and so they can't. So he's like kind of like hush hush conversations like oh what you're doing is fine like you should do this, but I can't say anything officially because my job would be at risk . . . I feel like they don't get to do what they want to do, because they have to pander to what the school wants them to do.

CSVAs were keenly aware of the many ways institutional power manifested in the parsing of information brought to bear on decision-making: who is (and is not) in the room/at the table when decisions are made and how messages about these decisions are communicated. They understood that each of these decision-making contexts shaped the ways an institution's sexual violence policies are considered, generated, and enforced.

Not surprisingly, they also recognized that as student activists, their positions weren't without power. Campus sexual violence activists recognized that they had the power to communicate institutional insolence, to publicly shame the institution and its leaders, and to tarnish the institution's brand.

CSVAs we interviewed understood themselves as both power*ful* (having the freedom to organize, speak, and express displeasure with the institution publicly and in high-profile ways), and power*less* (having little ability to truly impact policies and practices that directly affect them and their lives). They understood power as shifting and mercurial, its machinations subject to the decisions of those in formal positions of power, typically understood to be college administrators and to some extent, faculty. They were carried along by these shifts, vacillating from a sense of triumph, when a long-advocated policy change came to fruition, to the sting of impotence, when administrators refused a meeting or when their lists of urgently needed changes in practice were brushed aside or discounted. CSVAs recognized that institutional power is circulated among various actors on their campuses and is a governing characteristic of administrator-activist relationships. Generally, their experience of working with those in positions of power was disheartening, a place where the status quo generally ruled the day. Like activists in previous work, activists we interviewed "believed that administrators expected them to do all of the work in changing the system, since administrators were more invested in maintaining the current system than in changing it" (Ropers-Huilman, Carwile, and Barnett 2005, 302).

CSVAs' narratives revealed their deep awareness of the nature of institutional power, which Arendt (1998) gave particularly salient voice to:

Power's only limitation is the existence of other people, but this limitation is not accidental because human power corresponds to the condition of plurality to begin with. For the same reason, *power can be divided without decreasing it*, and the interplay of powers with their checks and balances is even liable to generate more power, so long, at least, as the interplay is alive and has not resulted in a stalemate. (201) [emphasis added]

Activists in this study recognized and resisted the zero-sum game equation related to institutional power. Consequently, they were rarely the source of stalemate situations. Instead, they gathered new momentum—sometimes in the form of new membership, other times in the form of new strategies—to continue to press institutions for change. In the face of institutional stalemates or intractability, CVSAs built new avenues of progress but returned again and again to peer relationships. CSVAs cultivated stronger, more authentic connections with other activists in order to steel themselves against the resistance or dismissal of institutional powerholders. Kate Lockwood Harris (2019, 19) has argued that while the focus is typically on individual acts of violence and the individuals who commit them, another form of violence—administrative violence—often accompanies it. The administrative violence affecting students is seen in institutional reporting systems (how institutions interpret and define sexual violence) that reinforce normative, racial, gender, and sexuality privileges and that attach little importance to the social and cultural influences that inform students' group experiences (Harris 2017).

For example, in a mandated system of reporting informed by gender, sexuality, and racial norms, characterizing an incident of sexual violence can lead to dismissing the incident and rejecting the claimant's experience. Students understood this, and in naming both the direct and indirect forms of administrative violence they and others experienced, they sought broader and more lasting remedies. They noticed (and named) also that their institutions work hard to obfuscate their role in perpetuating violence, preferring instead to reduce all acts to focusing on the harmed and the offender.

Institutional power operated in direct contrast to the creation and sustenance of relationships with institutional officers, and of trust building, ultimately compounding the harm of sexual violence on the campus community. These encounters generally served to amplify the subordination and lack of agency of the activists, a particularly troubling state of affairs when considering the common institutional discourses of commitment to community, caring, and student development in institutional mission statements. CSVAs demonstrated again and again that their power was primarily located in their solidarity with one another and their ability to continually regenerate new approaches and strategies from their collectivity.

However, the CSVAs that we interviewed felt that their activism has been unable to effectively jeopardize the institutional power that is circulated and guarded by its administrators and leaders. At times, as Rebecca remarked, institutional power was evident when administrators and leaders hid behind established processes that they controlled:

> *He reiterated that he felt that the processes that were in place were already fully equipped to handle all of these things (demands made by CSVAs) and no changes needed to be made. So he was like, "I sympathize, but I refuse to acknowledge that there's anything wrong."*

VOICING THE SILENCED

Despite frequent dismissals and silencing by campus administrators, CSVAs raised their voices to express displeasure with institutional leaders, with policies and practices, and with their deleterious effects, making public the institutional inaction and disregard. Making their grievances public effectively made their voices louder and imbued with greater power. While CSVAs used many avenues of expression to amplify their voices, more often than not social media were leveraged to communicate grievances against institutional practices and policies.

Like activists before them, CSVAs take their message to public spaces by organizing in-person protests and marches and by occupation of campus spaces. However, this generation of CSVAs circulates platforms, plans of action, membership drives, and safety information on Instagram, Facebook, and Twitter. Digital activism provides a space where CSVAs can and do control the narrative, both because of their relative agility in deploying messaging through online platforms and the ability to reach many more constituents than are possible through on-the-ground activism (Mendes Ringrose and Keller 2019, 185–186). Their dexterity in tactics was impressive. As Heldman, Ackerman, and Breckenridge-Jackson (2018) noted, the new generation of CSVAs uses "a sophisticated arrangement of formal political and legal tactics (lobbying, filing lawsuits, filing federal complaints, passing new laws, etc.) in tandem with unconventional political tactics (sit-ins, demonstrations, protests, online shaming campaigns, online petitions, etc.)" (67).

Social media are used by sexual violence activists to incite and energize student responses to incidents of rape and sexual violence and to document and hold institutions publicly accountable for forsaking students' safety on campus. In fall

2021 the *Chronicle of Higher Education* reported that students have used social media apps like GroupMe and YikYak to mobilize student protests against sexual violence and their "shrinking patience for the pace of change" on campus (Hidalgo Bellows, Brown, and Zaheis 2021), but social media have been deployed by campus sexual violence activists and advocates for some time (Linder et al. 2016). For example, Salter (2013) argues that social media enable dissemination of counter-hegemonic discourses, and girls and women have used these media to create fora for anti–sexual violence claims (203, 228–236). The analysis of narratives and affective vernacular practices on Tumblr and Twitter by Mendes et al. (2019) shows that online narratives of sexual violence have broad and critical effects: "These new digitized narratives not only shape what is disclosed and known about sexual violence, but what is felt and experienced, as they generate affective charges, for example, through the visceral creation of hand-crafted signs, or 'intimate publics' between those who use hashtags to connect their stories of sexual violence" (304).

Social media have become the "whisper networks," where students and student activists create public testimonies of their experiences of sexual violence to other students as a means to interfere with toxic campus cultures (Rentschler 2018, 505). These media extend and intensify messaging, helping to mobilize justice efforts on campus.

CSVAs recognized the power of amplifying their voices further when change was elusive, typically using social media. A social media campaign often led to a public protest, which led to occupation of campus spaces, which led to public scrutiny of institutions. Visibility through social media, campus media, and in some cases national media continued to turn up the pressure on administrators to think differently about policies and practices. Activists deployed volume and constancy to build exposure and calls for public accountability. But far from doing so to simply embarrass institutions, activists' tactics reminded other campus leaders of the strength and resilience of their commitment. They continually availed themselves of every outlet they could to hasten re-examination and change.

In the absence of being taken seriously, activists sought other forms of repair for their concerns, including the weight of the federal government's commitment to ensuring student safety. For example, in August 2021 a class action lawsuit, filed by four women students and alumnae on behalf of all women-identifying students at Brown from 2018 to the present was filed in federal court against Brown University. The lawsuit was unique in that it indicated that not only individual survivors but activists felt the brunt of the university's unresponsiveness: "Student activism such as the End Sexual Violence movement also encountered resistance from the University, the suit claims: Administrators only met with student activists after 'repeated requests' and implemented no 'material' changes" (Gupta and Kubzansky 2021). Such actions should serve as reminders that, while they were once limited to a phalanx of linked arms and placards, activists today use their voices in a wide variety of far more visible, impactful, and substantive ways to effect policy change and to do so through public exposure of institutional failings.

Backlash to social media posts is not uncommon (Anitha et al. 2020). CSVAs did not communicate any hesitancy to continue using social media strategically. CSVA social media campaigns were highly visible on campus and to broader publics, and yet activists did not share that they concerned themselves with backlash or legal retaliation. Rather they saw social media as a platform for survivor support and activism. For example, at Boston University, Yashica and other sexual violence activists gathered anonymous accounts of sexual violence experiences and then posted them on Instagram, where others provided supportive comments. Yashica explained:

> *I think our whole Instagram page is about supporting people and trying to bring them together and not only show that there is a problem, but also we hope to, in the future, work towards preventing that problem, reducing it, and turn into something that's actively creating change in a system that needs it.*

The CSVAs interviewed for this book recognize that social media are a means for survivors and women to retaliate against predators and institutions that enable predatory culture. A form of "feminist retaliation" (O'Donnell 2022), CSVAs make public institutional malaise about sexual violence and misogyny on social media. More importantly to CSVAs, by circulating an institution's inadequate and ineffective responses to survivor demands on social media, they were able to give voice to survivors' silence and shift shame from them onto their colleges and universities. As noted by O'Neill (2022), "With #MeToo, women found themselves newly empowered to shame (predators and sexual harassers)" (184). CSVAs understand that social media not only exposes institutional neglect and campus misogyny but allows survivors to transfer shame from themselves to predatory actors.

STRATEGY

Voice-raising via social media is a critical strategy used by activists working to end sexual violence on campuses. However, CSVAs use many other approaches. CSVAs develop and disseminate platforms; partner with supportive faculty, administrators, and alumni to advance their causes; make their demands known in loci of institutional power such as trustee meetings and faculty senates; and create inclusive fora for the advancement of their cause. In all cases, these activists centered survivors' narratives and experiences and infused their work with avowed intersectional consciousness. For example, survivors' voices were the primary focus in Nadia's efforts to create a support center at UMBC, in Anja's advocacy to eliminate the fee for transport to the local emergency room for survivors at Columbia, and in Kayla's reflection that one of the most important outcomes of her experience as an activist was being able to validate her own experiences as a survivor.

Intersectional thinking and collaboration were evident in Danu's outreach to Harvard College Democrats, the fossil fuel divestment group, and the Student Labor Action Movement urging them to show up for her group's protest actions (and they did). Intersectionality motivated Michelle's group's partnership with an LGBTQIA student group to cocreate educational efforts. It was visible in Morgan's insistence that trans Women of Color's needs must be centered in developing inclusive policies and services, and in Maya's commitment to centering Black women's voices in the coalition of students pushing for change at Georgetown.

These examples, nearly ubiquitous in our interviews, epitomize this generation of CSVAs' commitment to intersectional inclusivity in sexual violence activism. A commitment to intersectional frameworks shows up in the ideologies of those Conner (2020) termed "neoactivists," who "argue for a restructuring of the ways we consume, the ways we live our lives" (185). Awareness of intersectionality prompted white activists in other studies of CSVAs to step back from the dais to elevate other voices and their concerns (Marine and Trebisacci 2018, 659).

CSVAs' strategies often collided with the primary focus of most college administrators' compliance with Title IX. The emphasis on building a "culture of compliance," decried by Marine and Nicolazzo in 2017, has only increased, requiring those previously focused on guardianship of student safety to become experts in interpreting an obtuse (and ever-evolving) legal statute. Lee Burdette Williams (2015), a former senior administrator at two different colleges who has written extensively about her experiences navigating the complexities of Title IX work, described the frustration she experienced when the Department of Education released new guidance on how colleges must adjudicate sexual violence in 2011. She lamented:

> *I read the letter, nodding at some parts and shaking my head at others. It felt like a group of well-intended but misinformed interlopers had shown up to tell me how to do a job I had done for years. Absent any input from people in jobs like mine, this group of lawyers and policy specialists created a blueprint for an already existing structure, disregarding the years of effort undertaken to build it. We needed some renovation. They were requiring a gut rehab. . . . many of my counterparts and I had been doing the hard work of managing these cases for years and knew a lot about what worked well and what needed changing. Didn't our judgment, our input, count for anything?*

Williams' vexation at the continual flow of marching orders from the feds belied a larger conflict. When administrators' work is dictated primarily by federal policy, it appears to activists that they only care about protecting institutions from liability and in turn, protecting their jobs. While every campus has actors who will act from an impulse toward protecting institutional reputation over student safety, every campus also has principled, committed antiviolence educators, advocates, and their allies (Germain 2016, 100). The degree to which each type of professional is empowered, visible, and vocal typically shapes student experience, and the perpetuation or interruption of violence.

Stereotypes about campus policymakers' motivations and ethics render the various actors and their positions flattened, and troubling them is essential. Throughout the interviews with CSVAs, we saw heard evidence of activists' ability to hold multiple truths concurrently. Subhadra expressed this as follows:

> *[Having] fair policies doesn't mean they can't be neutral. . . . we want a fair process for everyone. But we're just asking the process not be unnecessarily hostile towards survivors. And so, I think there's a little bit of disconnect where they see us as survivor advocates, which we are, as wanting to somehow work this Title IX process.* But everyone loses when it's not a fair process. *[emphasis added]*

All of these efforts were challenged by COVID-19, which impacted the ways that activists thought and talked about strategy considerably. Our interviews with activists began in late fall 2019, extended through all of 2020, and concluded in early 2021. Consequently, we captured the intensity of not only particular iterations of activist movements but also the particularities of activism in the time of COVID. Students' strategies reflected a much stronger reliance on the internet, on electronic communication, and on gathering virtually; distance, and the negotiation of separation, permeated activists' actions and narratives. Most or all spoke wistfully of activism in real time, in close proximity to one another. Importantly, the loss of the ability to gather in person, while unfortunate, was not stultifying for activists in this study. Instead, it required creativity and a commitment to new and better approaches and ways of engaging. Activists' sense that momentum must be maintained permeated their stories and the stories of activism in the popular press (Jaisinghani 2020; Koller 2020; Zahneis and Patel 2020), reminding us again of their deep and unerring commitment even in the face of many unknowns.

Thus, power, voice, and strategy surfaced as formidable stress points on college activists opposing sexual violence. Time and time again in our study, we noted examples of activists' modifying their strategies when they encountered resistance or when their efforts were ignored. Their ingenuity, coupled with a steady commitment to building intersectional, communal approaches with other student groups typified their work. But their most formidable obstacle remained. Those who should logically be allies—student affairs practitioners—dismissed, ignored, or opposed their efforts.

STUDENT AFFAIRS PRACTITIONERS AND CAMPUS SEXUAL VIOLENCE CHANGE

Initially, we were puzzled by the sense that student affairs practitioners were perceived to be the greatest challenge to institutional change. As with CSVAs, committees, collaboration, and stakeholder inclusion are common features of the ways many student affairs practitioners often approach problem-solving on campuses (Manning, Kinzie, and Schuh 2012, 90). The profession is historically (and currently) organized around care for students, for their learning, and for their growth and development, and thus by definition their safety (ACPA and NASPA 2015). The shift from caretaker, committed to the fostering of growth and development, to regulatory compliance officer is deeply incongruous. We developed a deep sense of foreboding about this shift and about what it portends for the profession as a whole.

In true alignment with the history of the field, we urge a return to a focus on students and their well-being as the goal of student affairs work. Three specific factors drive us to this recommendation. First, a focus on student well-being corresponds more faithfully with student affairs' history of support, advancement, and solidarity with student activists. Second, student affairs practitioners are uniquely positioned to instigate changes to campus cultures and misaligned sexual violence practices and policies. Third, a focus on student well-being reflects the reality that student affairs practitioners are "ground zero" for advocacy for students' rights. First-year student advisors, multicultural support coordinators, sexual violence response center and peer educator coordinators, and all other student life officers are positioned by their institutions (and inspired by their professional mission) to advocate for students.

However, student affairs practitioners are obligated to serve the institution and are subordinates to institutional actors such as student affairs vice presidents and deans, presidents, and boards of trustees. As the CSVAs in our study observed, student affairs practitioners were simultaneously cooperative and unsympathetic; they were champions and obstructionists. They were employees who were conscious of their position in the institutional hierarchy, while also being power brokers to help move forward activist demands. Despite their awareness of student affairs practitioners' particular institutional position and relative institutional power, CSVAs believed that student affairs practitioners should serve as effective brokers for sexual violence activism. Despite the fact that CSVAs were frequently disappointed by student affairs practitioners' inaction, they looked to these practitioners as student advocates who could serve as agents for campus change by virtue of both their professional mission and their access to institutional power and decision-makers.

Given the nature of institutional power and decision-making, and the limits of student agency within it, CSVAs helped us understand that student affairs practitioners are ground zero in another sense. Student affairs practitioners are critical actors in developing and enacting a purposeful strategy to change institutional cultures that engender and support campus sexual violence. It is our contention that student affairs practitioners *must* serve as agents that broker collaboration between activists and other institutional leaders, centering relationality in their efforts to do so. Drawn from their long histories as advocates, this is a professional responsibility that is the key to changing campus cultures in allegiance with CSVAs.

STUDENT AFFAIRS' LEGACY OF ADVOCACY

The 1960s were a particularly fertile period for student activism on college campuses, and calls for greater equity and inclusion emerged from the civil rights movements of that era. College student affairs administrators were at the center of the work activists did to foment change (Gaston-Gayles et al. 2005). As individual leaders, operating within a system and bound by a set of ethical commitments their professional associations endorsed, these leaders were called to engage in the pressing issues of the era. However, their role was neither unequivocally to be an ally, nor to be an antagonist. As Augustine Pounds, an administrator at Oakland University in the 1960s who was often involved in responding to student racial equality activism, stated, "I had to decide how I would support students and how I could support my job responsibilities in order to keep my job.

I knew, early, that I could not be part of a system that denied me freedoms" (Wolf-Wendel et al. 2004, 332). Making such decisions was not without complexity, especially for former first-generation college students and administrators of color, such as Pounds.

Today, student affairs practitioners experience this tension inherent in their roles as both student advocates and compliant institutional officers. Student affairs practitioners are positional intermediaries between students and the institution and serve each set of institutional actors simultaneously. Responsible for students' development and quality of campus life and guided by a set of professional ethics (ACPA and NASPA 2015), they are employees of an institution and are bound by implicit and explicit assent and conformity to institutional power. As practitioners, they are obligated to serve two parties who are often at odds and that leverage very different forms of power. Activists use their power to make public institutional transgressions; colleges and universities can assert their power as employers. Consequently, student affairs practitioners are often targeted by their employers—including college presidents and trustees—to silence campus sexual violence activism and alleviate external threats such as litigation against the institution. For example, Melinda Manning, former assistant dean at the University of North Carolina, was pressured by UNC leadership to underreport sexual assault cases. According to a Title IX suit filed against the university in 2013,

> Manning was told by the University Counsel's office that the number of sexual assault cases she compiled for 2010 was "too high" before the total was decreased by three cases without her knowledge; that she was made the victim of a hostile work environment in the dean of students office; and

that her efforts to reform the University's handling of sexual assault cases were stymied more than once by higher administrators. (McCabe and Thomason 2013, 4)

Grievous harm is caused when institutions silence or penalize officers of their institutions who listen to campus activist students and work to openly address sexual violence. Not only will perpetrators go unpunished, but doing so suffuses the institution with a culture of permissiveness for violence (Sinko et al. 2021, 6). This manifests in many pernicious ways: pressure to protect a high-profile athlete whose performance on the field may generate sponsorship money for an institution (Dick and Ziering 2016), for example, or to protect the son of a local wealthy family (Baker 2017). But such actions often have a greater long-term cost: the continuation of a culture of violence, which (among other liabilities) exposes the institution to lawsuits brought by survivors.

Although the history of the profession of student affairs is replete with stories of administrators who have acted courageously, it sadly also includes institutional leaders who allow or encourage violence. For example, university president Grayson Kirk was inarguably responsible for the trauma unleashed on students involved in the 1968 Columbia University protest (Bradley 2010). Columbia's construction of a segregated gymnasium and its affiliation with defense projects associated with the Vietnam War fueled the massive student protest and occupation of campus administrative buildings. President Kirk responded to the student protest by filing trespassing charges against the students and bringing in the New York City police to clear the administrative buildings they occupied. The police brutalized students with physical force (e.g., beatings with nightsticks) and arrested hundreds of student protesters (McFadden 2005).

Kirk and others who allowed or encouraged violence side-step the reality that many student affairs practitioners have much in common with students who are sexual violence activists. As we heard from CSVAs, many express fidelity to their causes and have a deep sense of inability to effect change; they recognize their role in providing support and do their best to help students strategize for change. As colleges moved away from de jure *in loco parentis** in the 1970s, they inevitably hastened a shift to students wanting, and demanding, to take responsibility for their communities. Student affairs practitioners today must remain engaged in the complexities of the work to end sexual violence because they bring perspectives and insight that activists lack. However, their dual roles—as advocate, and as institutional officer—are by definition fraught. Research on administrators about their navigation of this complex challenge includes their passionately shared concern for student causes, and respect for the ways students embody them in their strategizing and action (Evans and Lange 2019, 71).

Evidence suggests that student affairs practitioners express their desire to demystify institutional politics and power to activists, even as they function within them (Markowitt 2009). Faculty and administrators thoughtfully recount ways they support activists in the day-by-day work of movement building, helping them to build confidence and grow in their ability to withstand the resistance they will face (Kezar 2010, 460–464). Acting as educators, advocates, counselors, mediators, and indeed, sometimes disciplinarians, student affairs practitioners *can* stand alongside activists and forge new bonds of

---

* *In loco parentis* refers to the generalized practice of treating college students as children, in the college's care "in place of parents." It was common practice in US colleges until the 1980s. For more on this subject, see William W. Cutler III, *Parents and Schools: The 150-Year Struggle for Control in American Education* (Chicago: University of Chicago Press, 2000).

trust and resistance together, according to research (Wolf-Wendel et al. 2004, 334–345). And perhaps most important, some student affairs practitioners are also survivors, whose own very personal suffering and healing inevitably shape and motivate their professional practices (Hurtado 2021).

The experiences with student affairs practitioners and faculty that CSVAs shared with us reflect the frustration of working with well-intentioned administrators who appear to be intent on changing the culture of sexual violence on campus, yet are unwilling to challenge the practices and policies that support and energize such a culture. Activists were often stonewalled by student affairs practitioners who themselves were fettered by institutional and career constraints. However, CSVAs also had experiences with administrators who took on powerful institutional actors on their behalf. Some CVSAs, like Morgan, Danu, and Michelle, especially valued and benefited from the learning relationships they had with administrators in women's centers, sexual violence response centers, and peer education programs.

At times, faculty played a pivotal role in supporting activists' causes. Andrea, Nadia, and Julia, among others, greatly valued the perspectives and counsel of faculty, who explained the conceptual frameworks and history that produce and sustain a culture of sexual violence inside and outside of campus. Though some faculty, like those at Stanford University, were more proactive and involved in changework, CSVAs did not consider them as key actors in their pursuit of sexual violence justice. Andrea appreciated that faculty at UNC "complained" about students' experiences and supported and accommodated her when she was diagnosed with posttraumatic stress disorder. Andrea found a faculty ally in the women's studies department who enacted curricular change to address sexual violence and saw her feminist faculty as the source of her intellectual growth and critical consciousness about gender violence. At Barnard College, Anja relied on faculty to serve as panelists to educate students on sexual assault. She described how she

> *organized a panel after the Brett Kavanaugh hearings to talk about what happened . . . to talk with faculty who knew more about how to analyze the issue and have more experience and have experience analyzing the Anita Hill hearing [and] could talk to members of the Barnard community so there could be dialogue and so people could open up about their feelings. And that was really cathartic and really rewarding.*

Like Andrea and many other activists, Anja relied on faculty's scholarly expertise and skills to educate other students and validate sexual violence activism on campus. However, like Danu and other activities, Anja recognized that though faculty's "capital" does afford them certain institutional power, faculty are often thwarted by administrative obstructions and their own professional goals. In the end, CVSAs recognized that even those faculty who campaigned for and championed their calls for institutional courage and responsibility would be thwarted by more powerful institutional inclinations.

COLLABORATION: REVISITING POWER, VOICE, AND STRATEGY

Inconsistent support from faculty and staff, as noted in CSVA narratives, and decades of viewing one another with suspicion and derision have curtailed the ability of activists, faculty, and administrators to collaborate and share power to end sexual violence. Certainly, there are examples of collaborative relationships between students, faculty, and staff forged by campus sexual assault education projects (Katz 2013, 656). Though these collaborative relationships broaden knowledge of sexual victimization on campus, they have not brought consensus on many issues (Katz 2013, 656). Alexandra Brodsky, former student activist and current civil rights attorney, expressed frustration with what she sees as the impasse between those who want fair and just policies and those who want justice for survivors. This impasse has led to unproductive disregard for the values inherent to both sides and the institution's refusal to share power with student activists (Brodsky 2016, 248).

The key to shifting this impasse is to return to a focus on relationality, to building better and stronger connections among parties of shared (and sometimes disparate) interests. Working to build relationality with those whom one ideologically opposes breaks down oppositional thinking ("this person is good, and this person is bad") and allows for new avenues of transformative action to emerge (Keating 2012). But doing so requires trust, and most of the CSVAs interviewed for this book admitted that they had not worked with or alongside relevant student affairs practitioners because they did not trust that they would be "seen" or "heard" by them. With the exception of a handful of women's center staff and a few feminist faculty, the vast majority of activists in our project could not name a single allied faculty or student affairs staff member that they saw as a partner/collaborator in the work.

Much of this is attributable to the phenomenon of compliance culture. As legal pressures have mounted, the work of campus sexual violence prevention and education has shifted to a focus on institutional liability and compliance. Activists, out of frustration with institutional stalemates and procedural preoccupation, turned away from the possibility of collaborative decision-making, instead employing more public strategies that called out institutional inaction and indolence. Student affairs practitioners charged with institutional compliance feel the increased pressure from their supervisors to give priority to compliance practices and policies, abdicating the institutional courage needed to address necessary culture change. But this, too, is a decision to disregard the need for institutional courage made by student affairs practitioners must be rectified.

MAKING THE CASE: BECOMING PARTNERS IN CHANGEWORK

We contend that the decision to forego working alongside activists is incongruous with the legacy and contemporary value sets of student affairs. Recently, the two most prominent student affairs professional organizations released statements calling for practitioners to recommit to social justice imperatives and to return their focus to the care of students. The American College Personnel Association / National Association of Student Personnel Administrators (ACPA / NASPA) Professional Competencies (2015) asserted that student affairs leaders must "Advocate on issues of social justice, oppression, privilege, and power that impact people based on local, national, and global interconnections . . . Advocate for the development of a more inclusive and socially conscious department, institution, and profession, and . . . Take responsibility for the institution's role in perpetuating discrimination or oppression" (30–31).

In a similar vein, ACPA–College Student Educators International (2019) has released a strategic plan on racial justice and decolonization that centers the very same intersectional commitment for social justice shared by CSVAs in this study. The statement specifically recognizes naming and eradicating all forms of violence as an essential challenge for student affairs.

Through these and other foundational documents, the profession has reasserted its commitment to naming and shifting power dynamics. Fostering a culture of respect and humanization is laudable, but what goes untroubled is the reality of distributive power that constrains the building of productive, collaborative relationships between activists and student affairs practitioners. Certainly, student affairs practitioners can become more receptive to building relationships with activists that can challenge problematic institutional discourses. By doing so, student affairs practitioners will fulfill the professional imperative to partner with the students, as outlined in the ACPA/NASPA principles. Recognizing that pragmatic action must be taken to change campus culture and the power of gender discourses, forging partnerships between student affairs practitioners and sexual violence activists could help bring about the necessary paradigmatic change activists call for.

Thankfully, there's a precedent for building this kind of fruitful partnership. In her 2010 article, "Faculty and Staff Partnering with Student Activists: Unexplored Terrains of Interaction and Development," Kezar explored the ways that partnerships can foster change on college campuses as well as the development of student learning and growth. She found that faculty and staff committed to working with student activists to foster their growth and development did so in a number of ways: (a) embedding their support in a larger educational opportunity, like teaching a class or service learning opportunity with and for student activists; (b) helping students negotiate effectively with senior administrators; (c) mentoring activists around strategy and approach, and in some cases, (d) directly participating in protests and other public actions. Kezar borrowed Meyerson's framing of these actors as "tempered radicals," defined as "individuals who identify with and are committed to their organizations, and are also committed to a cause, community, or ideology that is fundamentally different from, and possibly at odds with the dominant culture of their organization" (Meyerson and Scully 1995, 586). Kezar's (2010) work is evidence that activists and student affairs practitioners need not be in constant conflict; that "important student development seems to occur through faculty/staff partnering with students in activism and bottom-up leadership" (474). Undoubtedly, fostering this development is the primary focus of the student affairs profession.

COLLABORATIVE RELATIONSHIPS AND COLLABORATIVE POWER

Student activists' understanding of power, voice, and strategy richly informed the ways they think about the value of collaborative relationships with student affairs practitioners for ending sexual violence on college campuses. To develop and engage in collaborative relationships it is critically important that activists and student affairs practitioners engage in (a) table setting, (b) naming the competing tensions, (c) naming the limits of compliance culture, and (4) moving beyond compliance to transformation.

Table setting. Throughout this book, activist narratives are replete with examples of administrators, faculty, or both developing policies and practices without including or consulting with student activists. This practice resulted in deep mistrust, as students recognized that their calls for change were being dismissed, and so they often reacted with public critique. It is our contention that, quite simply, *no policy or practice related to opposing campus sexual violence should be developed, vetted, or considered final until students, specifically student activists, are at the table and part of collaborative deliberations.* This practice will result in more effective and successful policymaking because it is informed by student experience and student perspective. It does not mean students write, or have sole and final say over policies, because that would also sidestep the power of collaboration. Student affairs practitioners bring meaningful and important perspectives to the conversation, but theirs are not the only or most meaningful perspectives in every case.

An excellent example of collaborative table setting is developing response protocols and practices on campuses, in which student advocates train with a state-supported rape crisis protocol. In these cases, students are treated as essential and indispensable participants. As CSVAs in our study noted, institutions that resist students being at the table are inevitably setting themselves up for student discontent and public shaming by student activists. Bringing student activists to the table, setting ground rules together for how policies will be reviewed and developed, listening carefully to their concerns, and working together to create inclusive policies is a more productive and justice-oriented approach that will benefit both students and the institution.

To build collaborative relationships, participants must *name the tensions experienced by the institution.* As a routine part of table setting, student affairs practitioners must work to ensure that student activists fully understand the pressures bearing down on all institutions related to Title IX compliance. This means understanding that Title IX compliance is not the end goal, but rather a starting point for effective policymaking, and requires helping students understand the federal government's role and evolution in regulating Title IX policy and regulations, and the institution's liability. It also demands that institutional officers ensure that students understand the relationship between Title IX compliance and the institution's ability to en-

sure that federal financial aid and research funding will be com-
promised if Title IX compliance law is disregarded.

Helping students understand Title IX, their rights and responsibilities under Title IX, and the institution's role in ensuring compliance is a reality-based approach that allows students
to better understand the policy positions taken by institutions.
Students will be in a better position to name the aspects of Title
IX that are student-unfriendly and work with institutions and
their governmental relations staff to continue to press to transform these particular regulations. Further, as Harris (2019) has
argued, a sole focus on the observance and enforcement of Title
IX allows institutions to sidestep the harder work of rooting out
ways that institutions promote and proliferate violence through
other discursive practices. It allows for the larger cultural forces
(misogyny, racism) at work on each campus to be elided, while
focusing solely on finding bad actors and holding them accountable. Partnership with activists will keep the larger cultural issues
that support sexual violence under constant scrutiny and will
ideally generate better thinking about how to address them.

Student affairs practitioners must embrace their roles as both
educators *and* advocates. Thus, in addition to familiarizing student activists with Title IX regulations, student affairs practitioners must *listen* to the realities of students' everyday experiences
on their campus. CSVAs reminded us that being a student on
each campus is an experience that only students can name and
describe; the native wisdom they bring to the larger facets of
culture change work cannot be supplanted with the (presumed)
more advanced understanding of administrators. This work
will not be easy or comfortable. Administrators including (but
not limited to) women's center and crisis center staff, and faculty
must listen closely to students' recounting of their experiences

with harassment and violence, and the impact of the resulting trauma they experience. Understanding survivor trauma and the effects of a campus culture that supports and enables violence in multiple forms is a necessary condition of collaborative relationships with student activists.

Purposeful and effective collaborative relationships between student sexual violence activists and student affairs practitioners are a necessary condition for building the institutional courage necessary to change the cultures of gender violence on our campuses. Institutional courage is "an institution's commitment to seek the truth and engage in moral action, despite unpleasantness, risk, and short-term cost. It is a pledge to protect and care for those who depend on the institution. It is a compass oriented to the common good of individuals, institutions, and the world. It is a force that transforms institutions into more accountable, equitable, effective places for everyone" (Center for Institutional Courage n.d.).

Practicing institutional courage will require student affairs practitioners and campus leaders to exercise leadership with integrity for the student activists in their care. Leadership with integrity demands that institutional leaders examine their motives, assumptions, and beliefs about activists and act with a spirit of collaboration toward them. Committing to this will inform student affairs practitioners about the everyday realities of campus life for students and attune administrators to their concerns. The native experts, student activists, can provide crucial context for the ways that policies and practices play out and how students will respond to them.

LIMITS OF COMPLIANCE CULTURE

At the beginning of this chapter, we presented a case for the power and value of imagination in building and developing new ways of thinking about ending sexual violence. Nowhere is this more urgent than in the ways that we understand and talk about justice and accountability for perpetrators. Each time a US president and secretary of education release a new set of rulings regarding adjudication, college leaders scramble to fall in line with the most recent edicts, replacing all creativity and concern for the welfare of survivors and perpetrators alike. Our contention of imperative collaborative relationships with student activists rests on several different assumptions, but most principally on the assumption that together, activists and administrators can devise new and better ways to hold perpetrators accountable within the boundaries of Title IX and its federal requirements. Title IX is simply a starting point, the minimum a college or university must do. Reaching beyond to infuse the work of culture change with new thinking and conceptual foundations, especially for accountability, is imperative.

On campuses across the United States, activists and student affairs practitioners are working collaboratively on both restorative and transformative justice. Brown University, and the leadership of its Office on Transformative Justice (Bautista 2020), is an example of the ways that institutions can provide opportunities to think differently and collaboratively about perpetrator accountability and the ways to reintroduce a perpetrator into a community of caring others. Transformative justice aims to restore and address harm through community processes, centering the survivor but also acknowledging the community-based nature of the harm. Restorative and transformative justice approaches replace the adversarial, courtroom-based option common in most college and university sexual violence policies with a more holistic, community-centered, and reparative approach to the problem.

Alletta Brenner (2013) has made the case for the potential of restorative and transformative justice approaches on college campuses. Brenner has argued that numerous features of campus adjudication approaches typically performed as courtroom-like, adversarial processes render them ineffective. Among these flaws, Brenner notes, are the ways that such processes emphasize individual acts of violence, rather than the need for a cultural change. These processes rarely hold offenders accountable. Rarely do survivors choose to avail themselves of these processes. Further, they don't attend to dialogue that is necessary between parties who will remain members of the same campus community after the regulatory processes have concluded (Brenner 2013, 3–9). Adopting a different stance will require administrators to become receptive to building authentic collaborative relationships with activists and to listen with a different mindset. As Murphy and Van Brunt (2016) explained, "It is important to find ways to engage with these [activist] organizations and understand what goals and priorities they have. Campus administrators can easily misstep because of adversarial relationships or concern about neutrality related to controversial efforts, but it is quite possible to partner with these groups on common goals and priorities" (257–258).

Restorative and transformative justice policies and practices must also contend with a perpetrator's denial and disavowal of responsibility. Both restorative justice and transformative justice practices must contend with perpetrators' spurious excuses and explanations that shift the blame away from themselves and onto victims (Wegner et al. 2015). CSVAs echoed this concern and believe it is essential to hold perpetrators truly accountable and responsible in restorative and transformative practices.

In *Beyond Nassar: A Transformative Justice and Decolonial Feminist Response to Campus Sexual Assault*, Xhercis Méndez (2020) reminded us that "Title IX compliance was never the end goal" (88). Instead, she argued that we should be working toward "[recognizing] that the system that has been set up to extract 'justice' through a criminal justice modality has also created the very conditions that make it less likely that those who have caused or enabled harm will voluntarily step into and take responsibility for their actions" (90). Alternatively, Méndez argued that the billable hours expended in fighting an institution's legal liability and putative failures to enact Title IX appropriately could be usefully redirected to explore the many ways institutions could enact more just, inclusive, and fair processes of accountability to harm repair. Such practices would not only provide more imaginative approaches to healing harm but would honor the intersectional social justice goals prioritized by sexual violence activists in this study. CSVAs concerned themselves with the many ways that institutional systems of justice must factor the ways that queer, trans, and survivors of color experience sexual and/or gender-based violence.

FROM COMPLIANCE TO TRANSFORMATION

Finally, to establish productive and effective collaborative relationships and for true transformation to happen, all parties must agree on the criteria for assessment, the means of assessment, and the parameters for accountability. In the experiences CSVAs shared with us, we noticed that CSVAs viewed institutional leaders' values (professed or observed) as directly conflicting with their own. While each was concerned about creating change, activists sensed that faculty and administrators cared primarily about managing the problem rather than confronting it directly through an unflinching examination of the campus culture.

In place of assumptions about the nature of student culture, drinking behaviors, or the role of athletes and fraternities, activists named a need to assess all of these features collectively (and to better understand how they work in tandem) to understand the nature of the problem and whether progress was being made. Activists perceived "management" of the problem to be meaningless reform and wanted nothing short of an eradication of gender and sexual violence as the goal. But they were not unrealistic about this: they recognized and named the uphill nature of the work. They spoke of building new and better strategies to address it, which they viewed as typically out of reach because of administrator stalemates.

While students on each campus are the best source of thinking about the specific kinds of changework needed, at least one promising model for advancing and assessing campus efforts to eradicate sexual violence exists. The model, developed by Luoluo Hong (both an activist and a senior student affairs administrator), acknowledges and addresses the reality of responding to current incidents while culture change is underway. Hong's (2017) social justice paradigm "challenges educators to move beyond the rhetoric of prevention conflated with efforts to improve the institutional response to a comprehensive approach that engenders transformational change . . . the paradigm incorporates a systemic set of sustained initiatives to address sexual violence on multiple levels, moving beyond traditional notions of how to do sexual violence work" (31).

Hong's model revises the traditional sexual violence paradigm on college campuses by distributing responsibility for addressing sexual violence *across an institution,* substituting preoccupation with individual incidents with a broader focus on cultural change (table 1). Hong presents a model that is intersectional, inclusive of student concerns and energies, and equally invested in prevention and response work. It is pragmatic but visionary; it is imaginative but grounded. In a follow-up essay regarding the nature of the work, Hong named several institutions, including Emory University, Harvard University, and San Francisco State

TABLE 1: Revised Traditional and Social Justice
Paradigms for Sexual Violence Prevention
(Hong and Marine 2018)

TRADITIONAL PARADIGM	SOCIAL JUSTICE PARADIGM
Focuses primarily on individual responsibility (usually that of the victim, as well as that of the bystander)	Focuses on individual actions plus systemic/cultural factors, institutional policies, political context, and their interrelationship
Agency of the perpetrator is largely invisible or unacknowledged	Agency of the perpetrator and the system that supports their actions is named and made transparent
Does not acknowledge the salience of identity, power, and privilege in human interactions	Intersections of identity, power, and privilege are essential to understanding and deconstructing interpersonal dynamics
Violence and its prevention are defined from the perspective of and controlled by the dominant group	The *single story* is challenged, and understandings of violence are complex and informed by many counter narratives
Peer health educators implement programming	Peer health leaders are embedded in existing social groups
Prevention work tends to occur in isolation; efforts are fragmented and inconsistent	Prevention work is infused across multiple entities working collaboratively to build and sustain community capacity
Focuses almost exclusively on transactional effectiveness	Focuses on transformational and transactional impact
Is an overlay on the institution's existing practices, programs, policies, and procedures	Infiltrated and disrupts systems, structures, culture, and core values of the institution
Relies primarily on insight, looking to the campus for sources of knowledge, expertise, answers, and solutions	Relies on both insight and outsight, looking in all places for answers as well as collaborating to create new knowledge
Sustained as long as the *champion* is present	Sustainable over time, with many champions
Requires care and competence	Requires care, competence, and moral courage

University, where elements of the model are already in place (Hong and Marine 2018).

Fully embracing the social justice paradigm rather than sole compliance with Title IX assessments promises to bring new opportunities for transformation and for activist–student affairs practitioner collaboration. This strategy promises to enable a broader range of stakeholders to engage in the work, allowing for a generation of new and better technologies for transforming cultures that foment and support violence. It can enable rebuilding trust between activists and their administrator-allies, because the focus will shift away from compliance and toward meaningful, lasting changework. Use of the social justice paradigm promises to close the chasm that has worn over time between stakeholders and enable the difficult, but essential manifesting of institutional courage.

However, this tactic will require bold and decisive action by senior as well as less-seasoned student affairs practitioners; they will be called to engage with other leaders at their institutions and to push back on narratives that center compliance. They will be called to forge new avenues of understanding and allegiance with activists, toward the only defensible goal: not simply complying with Title IX regulations, or avoiding costly and embarrassing public lawsuits, but ending campus sexual violence permanently.

Chapter 6

A CULTURAL RESET

In 2017 widespread and unchecked sexual misconduct in Hollywood was brought into public view by the *New York Times* reporters Jodi Kantor and Megan Towhey and the *New Yorker* investigative reporter Ronan Farrow (Farrow 2017; Kantor and Towhey 2017). Their exposés revealed a culture of sexual predation in which rich and powerful men in the television and motion picture industry sexually assaulted women and silenced them through intimidation and coercion. Long suspected of sexual predation, Hollywood producer Harvey Weinstein was publicly implicated in rape allegations and eventually criminally charged. Though only six women testified at his trial, many more raised similar allegations against Weinstein. Galvanized by the Weinstein case and public outcry, actor Alyssa Milano adopted Tarana Burke's #MeToo hashtag to encourage survivors of sexual assault to be acknowledged and to be heard. This act of "naming and shaming" was seen as feminist whistleblowing on an industry's widespread and enduring culture of sexual violence; it was a moment when "a digital and networked *parrhesia*" served as declaration of the "open secret" of the culture of sexual violence (Dos Santos Bruss 2019, 725).

At the conclusion of Harvey Weinstein's trial in February 2020, Farrow interviewed actor-survivor Rose McGowan, asking what the verdict meant to her and to other sexual violence survivors. For McGowan, the verdict was a personal victory for her and for all those who were violated by Weinstein, but also for all survivors of sexual assault who had been silenced. McGowan reflected that her decision in 2016 to tweet about her sexual assault and then go on the record about her 1997 assault by Weinstein was a desire for a "cultural reset" (Farrow 2020).

McGowan's "cultural reset" was a call to extend #MeToo's culture of survivor empowerment to a different practice that names perpetrators of rape and sexual violence publicly in order to disempower them. For McGowan, publicly naming rapists on Twitter was a way to "take a big sword" and "cut off the head of power" (Farrow 2020); it was a means to reset the culture of sexual assault hashtag activism to an activist culture that aims to disenfranchise the institutional, economic, and social power of perpetrators. For example, by naming perpetrators publicly on social media, she directed culpability to them, requiring that they, and not survivors, be the objects of cultural shame, humiliation, and public scrutiny. McGowan reminded us that rape and sexual assault are a manifestation of a culture in which power and masculinity are constructs and discourses that reinforce each other, and in which "rape cultures" are supported by institutional practices and policies.

McGowan's "cultural reset" is C. Christine Fair's (2017) call for acknowledging that rape and sexual assault are a manifestation of cultures of power and masculinity. In Fair's rendering of her experiences with sexual assault and sexual harassment in academia, she names perpetrators and experiences and situates them in institutional cultures at Yale, the University of Chicago, and Harvard University. Fair (2017) critiques #MeToo and other hashtag activism for keeping the "onus" on "victims to stand up and once again be counted." Instead, Fair would rather see social media posts by *perpetrators* who would confess the seriousness and significance of their predation on their victims' lives.

Fair's suggested upending of sexual assault hashtag activism resonates with the cultural reset demanded by McGowan. It is likely that McGowan and Fair would rather a see a sea change in sexual violence hashtag activism that shifts the onus to perpetrators and not survivors. Unlike survivor testimonies on Twitter or other social media, confession by perpetrators and not testimony by survivors would shift the moral imperative to perpetrators. Though the value of LoSHA (List of Sexual Harassers in Academia) and other published lists of sexual predators is that they generate public discussion about allegations of sexual violence and harassment (Anitha et al. 2020), especially in communities where survivors are silenced and a culture of silence dominates, Fried and McGowan would argue that these reflect cultures in which the responsibility for reporting, making public, and giving witness to sexual violence still resides with survivors. Though powerful and meaningful to survivors, these do not reset the culture of sexual violence nor change expectations to hold perpetrators accountable.

The accounts of campus sexual violence activism shared with us by campus sexual violence activists echoed McGowan's and Fair's scrutiny of the cultures and discourses that promote sexual violence and sexual harassment on campus. At a demonstration on the University of Massachusetts's Amherst campus in fall 2021, survivors and allies demonstrated against the "culture of rape, harassment, and secrecy" at the university (Carlin, Stoico, and Alanez 2021), a culture that students and survivors know supports the campus party scene and fraternity misbehavior. The university's failure to acknowledge how "rampant" sexual assault is on campus is viewed by survivors and allies as fundamental to the institution's culture that facilitates sexual violence and ignores calls for substantive institutional cultural change (Carlin, Stoico, and Alanez 2021). The CSVAs in our study testified that their institutional cultures are also sustained by discourses of power and gender that render much of their activism impotent and they repeatedly challenge campus leaders to bring about a cultural reset on campus. They frequently spoke of the cultures of masculinity and power that were discursive on their campuses. These discourses animated institutional support—whether explicit or implicit—for undergraduate alcohol-fueled party cultures, predacious fraternities, and institutional immunity for male athletes accused of sexual violence. As in the case of UMass Amherst, the CSVAs in our study recognized that these discourses prevent administrators from seeing the need for extending the range of services for survivors and allow them to resist the calls for change.

INSTITUTIONAL CULTURE, INSTITUTIONAL POWER

As institutional betrayal theorist and scholar Jennifer Freyd has noted (Bartlett 2021), institutions resist the cultural resets called for by campus sexual assault activists because institutions look to safeguard the status quo in order to maintain traditional discourses of power.

Consequently, sexual violence in universities can be understood as the point of intersection for gendered norms and relations of power within the institution. As Davids (2020) asserted, gender-based violence in universities is "as much about the entrenchment of hegemonic norms, as it is about a need for the disruption of the structures and discourses sustaining these norms" (13). The entrenchment of hegemonic gender norms in higher education has not gone unexamined by scholars (e.g., Lester and Sallee 2017; Martínez Alemán 2014; Acker and Dillabough 2007), but how do these norms create and perpetuate the structures that curb campus sexual assault activists' calls for cultural reset on campus?

As institutions, US colleges and universities are social organizations connected to the just and social good in a democratic society. This overarching mission is the activist's foothold for changing campus cultures. Public or privately held, colleges and universities are organizations that contribute to the public good (Gumport 2000), a good that has historically included individual development and social and economic mobility (Cohen and Kisker 2010). As neoactivists, CSVAs in our study believed that their colleges and universities have a social responsibility to those they educate (Conner 2020, 185). Like the activists at the UMass Amherst rally in 2021, CSVAs in our study understand that the university has "the responsibility" and "the moral obligation" to create an environment—a campus culture—in which all students can "safely live and learn" (Carlin, Stoico, and Alanez 2021). The CSVAs we interviewed contended that their institution's adherence to gender norms that nurture and favor unsafe campus environments epitomized by party culture and unfettered fraternity conduct clearly compromises individual student development and discredits the institution's social mission. Student's psychological and physical safety is correlated with sexual violence on campus, and as the University of Nebraska's Black Student Union president reflected, "If students don't feel safe on campus, . . . then that means that there's a deep problem" (Hidalgo Bellows et al. 2021).

The deep problem perceived by campus survivors, sexual violence activists, and allies is rooted in higher education's gendered structures and misogynistic cultures and the maintenance of discourses of power that limit structural changes in the status quo. Throughout their histories, institutions of higher education as organizations have been organized based on socio-cultural norms in which gender power and gender privilege create and preserve women's inequality (Acker 1990, 2006).

The rise of neoliberal ideals in higher education today has fortified and enhanced those gender discourses that accentuate masculinity as higher education's organizing principle (Martínez-Alemán 2014). The neoliberal university has reinvigorated distributive, hierarchical power that has enabled a more individualistic view of campus sexual assault that ignores the structural and institutional cultures that foment sexual assault on campus (Phipps 2018). As Phipps (2018) observed, the UK's "lad culture" (71) is symptomatic of the intersections between discursive masculinity and neoliberalism, cultural junctions at which men's misogynistic behavior is normed. Like the CSVAs we interviewed, British activists form coalitions to resist these norms and find that their institutions ignore women's experiences in lad cultures (Lewis, Marine, and Kenney 2018). In the United States, it is at this normative intersection we can see misogynistic athletic culture (MacGregor 2018) and fraternity cultures that sanction violence against women (Seabrook, Ward, and Giaccardi 2018; Seabrook, McMahon, and O'Connor 2018).

As an organization, the university's culture will consequently empower attitudes and gender inequality in which sexual violence is one of its manifestations. As Schein (1991) noted, all organizations have a culture that socializes relationships, establishes processes, and embeds structures based on dominant norms. In the case of colleges and universities, like many other organizations, the power and privilege given to masculinity constitutes the organizational "regimes" (Acker 1990, 146) that engender and perpetuate gender sexual and violence culture. Scholars have examined the varieties and complex nature of masculinity as both a cultural construct and a source of sexual violence. Though the many types of masculinity may manifest in different ways, they are all derivative of organizations' contexts and cultures (Morris and Ratajczak 2019). Harris's (2017, 2019) examinations of universities' responses to rape and its processes to address sexual violence assert that institutions' systemic attitudes and ideals are animated and guided by race (whiteness), gender (masculinity), and sexuality (heteronormativity). More important, Harris submits that universities are culpable actors in campus sexual violence because of their discursive adherence to racial, gender, and sexuality norms.

An institution's discursive nature (expressed through official leadership statements, policies, and other campus communications) is a primary way through which relations of power throughout its organization are sustained and replicated. The relations of power in the university can thus be understood as "structured social practice" through which meaning is given to different experiences in the organization, which are then systematically privileged or disregarded. Consequently, the university's discursive underpinning is a "process of signification" that "functions to structure systems" such that "certain conceptions of reality are organized into everyday practices, while other possible conceptions are organized out" (Mumby and Stohl 1991, 314). The dominance and privileging of the masculinities in the university, especially as these pertain to sexual violence, reflect the relations of power that conserve campus policy and practices that frustrate and obstruct sexual violence activism. Investing more in protection of its brand maintenance through heightened scrutiny and investment in compliance functions, the neoliberal institution has heightened preexisting power inequalities between institutional leaders and student affairs practitioners, diminishing their capacity for proactive anti–sexual violence action.

Not unsurprisingly then, CSVAs' calls for change in policy and practice are met with discursive resistance by university officials and practitioners, a universal phenomenon encountered by gender equality activists worldwide (Laoire et al. 2021). As whistleblowers, CSVAs speak truth to power that is incompatible with organizational cultures derived from a discourse that endows power and privilege to those experiences that replicate and emulate gender hierarchies. Essentially, campus sexual violence is a manifestation of the institution's discursive heart. Therefore, attempts to alter its structured social policies and practices challenge the institution's conceptualizations of reality—what behaviors are privileged and acceptable, what experiences are brushed away or silenced. These attempts are met with discursive or conceptual and cultural resistance and intransigence that the CSVAs in our study experience as palpably exhausting, rendering their efforts fruitless.

The overarching nature of gender and power informs the campus experience so that sexual violence is viewed as matter of institutional compliance with laws and federal government mandates and not as a symptom of institutional culture. The experiences of the CSVAs in our study support this. To date, changes in institutional reporting policies on sexual violence and practices, the establishment of required sexual violence/harassment/assault education programs for students, and legislated progressive changes to federal directives have failed to deliver a cultural reset on campus, making sexual violence activism ultimately ineffectual. The CSVAs in our study acknowledged that compliance policies and practices are certainly necessary—they are the minimum needed to combat sexual violence on campus—but do little to undo the institutional gender norms that allow fraternity, athletics, and alcohol-fueled party cultures that are ground zero for sexual assault and rape.

An institution's failure to prevent sexual assault or respond compassionately to survivors of campus sexual violence often results in survivors feeling "betrayed" by their college or university, an institution they depend upon. The institutional betrayal felt by survivors of campus sexual violence is (in part) the result of poor or inadequate institutional responses to sexual violence (Smith and Freyd 2013), a theme common in the CSVAs' testimonies. However, like the CSVAs testified, the institution's failure to protect survivors from sexual violence is the more salient aspect of the betrayal. How institutions create and then support a campus environment conducive to sexual assault exacerbates survivors' feelings of betrayal by the institution they trust (Smith and Freyd 2013, 122–123). Consequently, the institutional discourses that produce, deepen, and sustain campus environments prone to sexual assault and violence are a source of these betrayals. The CSVAs in our study saw how student affairs practitioners were largely powerless to direct and enact proactive change that targeted these betrayals.

During his tenure as vice president, Joe Biden asserted at Morehouse College that sexual violence on campus is "a cultural problem" (Davis 2015). Six years later, as president, Biden ordered the US Department of Education to re-examine the former administration's rulings in campus sexual violence (Rogers and Green 2021) and Title IX enforcement (Gravely 2021). At Morehouse College, Biden asserted that rape and sexual violence as "a cultural problem" is imbedded in "the standard of decency by which we measure ourselves" (Davis 2015). Though arguably attempts both to change the culture of rape and to empower victims through legislative acts and appeal to moralities are laudable, neither gets at the heart of the matter, that is, the need for institutions *themselves* to undo discourses of gender inequality conducive to sexual violence.

At Morehouse, a historically Black men's college, Biden called upon college students everywhere to change the culture of sexual violence on their campuses to a culture in which there is no tolerance for sexual violence. As discourses that compose rape cultures on college campuses, both masculinity and power are also raced and racialized and are imbued and animated by narratives of race (Grundy 2021, 243–244). Consequently, codified acceptable sexual behavior and gender expectations operate (in part) to make possible rape cultures on college campuses that are raced and racialized. The CSVAs in our study recognized that race was an integral element of toxic campus cultures, something absent in Biden's call for a cultural reset at Morehouse and elsewhere.

The CSVAs we interviewed view these calls for change at the hands of activist students as missing the point, and a symptom of the true source of the problem. The problem lies with the college or university's culture of gender inequality. Sexual violence is one manifestation of that culture. Hence, in order to achieve Biden's "zero tolerance" for sexual violence, the college itself must reset its discourses and structures of gender inequality. Like Biden's, generic calls for cultural change ignore the history of gender and its complex relationship with the machinations of power that involve many other forms of sub-jugation, especially racial objectification.

INSTITUTIONAL CHANGE
AND CULTURAL RESET

To reset the culture of sexual violence, CSVAs argued that in-stitutions must eradicate the discursive support for predatory cultures on campus and privilege survivor empowerment in their practices. Though activists recognize that institutional compliance with federal laws and mandates does provide survi-vors with avenues for justice, they are also keenly aware that their colleges and universities have fixated on compliance prac-tices at the expense of changing the culture of sexual violence on campus. CSVA experience with student affairs practitioners does serve as evidence that, in their preoccupation with meeting federal compliance obligations, institutional leaders have trun-cated student affairs' institutional and professional power. In the eyes of the CSVAs in our study, institutional leadership thwarts or outright forbids the proactive efforts of student affairs prac-titioners to execute policies aimed at curbing misogynist dis-courses that fuel fraternity, athletic, and party cultures on cam-pus (Marine and Nicolazzo 2017). By limiting student affairs practitioners solely to compliance practices and compliance re-porting, institutional leaders have encumbered the ability of stu-dent affairs practitioners to empower and care for activists them-selves. Their vocational authority hamstrung by the emphasis on compliance and institutional leaders' power to authorize and com-mand such focus on compliance, student affairs practitioners can't stay true to their professional history, mission, and ethics.

Institutional preoccupation with Title IX compliance has effectively neutralized the vocational and positional power of

student affairs practitioners to bring about activist empowerment. In doing so, institutions have handicapped proactive action that could change predatory culture on campus. Originally
hired by institutions to serve as "enforcers and overseers rather
than professional helpers" (Thelin 2018, 86–87), student affairs
transformed into a profession charged with caring for students
"at all junctures of a student's college experience" (Thelin 2018,
113). In their years as the on-the-ground authorities responsible
for monitoring and adjudicating student misconduct, student
affairs personnel served to preserve the integrity of institutional
policies first. As the profession evolved, a more student-
centric student development mission became the centerpiece
of the profession. This transformation, not surprisingly, also
served the institutional brand and position in the marketplace
of the era. As institutions faced the need to offer more regulatory practices on and compliance reporting of sexual harassment, sexual violence, and other gendered harms, student affairs practitioners charged with sexual violence education and
transformation of misogynist student cultures found themselves
retreating from their earlier professional purposes. The institutional pressure to focus primarily on compliance has reverted
their work to student surveillance and misconduct reporting of
an earlier era.

The discursive power of misogyny animates sexual violence
on campus. Misogyny, as gendered power, permeates the institutional policies and practices so that sexual violence and harassment are normalized. Despite the decades of empirical research
that has pointed to their perpetuation of sexual violence and
gender objectification, fraternities are still commonplace on college and university campuses. Men's athletics, frequently a location of gender-based and sexual violence, is still privileged
on many campuses, and men who are athletes are privileged and

protected by institutional leaders. The consumption of alcohol and the prevalence of party cultures on campuses continue unabated, despite the fact that these student cultures create the predatory conditions for sexual violence (Davis et al. 2018). And yet, as research has shown (and as our activists confirmed through their testimonials), institutional leaders fixate on compliance policies and practices and the expense of empowering professionals to educate for cultural reset on campus. As Marine and Nicolazzo (2017) noted, institutions fail students, erroneously believing that "by focusing on compliance, higher education administrators can advance liberation and social justice, especially in relation to sexual violence on college campuses. By knowing, and enforcing, particular mandates issued by the federal government, violence committed by students against other students will be abated, as if the root cause of such violence is in fact a poor understanding of law."

Compliance policies and practices are a reality for institutions, certainly. However, if colleges and universities are to reset the culture of sexual violence, they must be willing to self-consciously examine the larger cultural forces at play. But because institutional power is gendered, institutional leadership is incapable of engaging in an ecology of action that is necessary to reset the culture of sexual violence on their campuses. We heard from CSVAs that what is needed is proactive cultural change and not just reactive institutional action (compliance). Professional organizations like the Association of American Universities (AAU) have taken these activist demands to heart and have called for institutions to create campus climates where sexual violence and harassment are objectionable and counternormative (Carrasco 2021). College presidents have voiced antipathy for predatory culture on their campuses responsible for sexual violence and degradation (Jaschik 2021). For example,

Ana Mari Cauce, President of the University of Washington, called on her campus community to acknowledge that ending sexual violence and sexual harassment requires building a campus culture that does not accept gender cruelty as normative, and that "deliberate and concerted leadership" is required to provoke and support such cultural change (Cauce 2018).

Because undoing discursive misogyny is a herculean undertaking, a more pragmatic approach is necessary to engage proactively to affect a cultural reset on campus. What the experiences and perceptions of CSVAs suggest to us is that proactive action can begin by empowering student affairs practitioners to work *with* student activists to enact change. This will mean, of course, that institutional leaders must commit to permitting and enabling student affairs practitioners to return their focus to impacting campus culture by attending to the education and development of students. This will require institutional leaders to hold firm on their commitment to compliance policy and reporting *and* to empower student affairs practitioners to broaden their professional work and action to tackle (first) those student spaces (e.g., athletics, fraternities, party culture) where sexual violence is unbridled. Institutional leaders must recognize this as a way to direct and achieve stated institutional goals of serving and educating all students equitably. Institutional leaders must also recognize that narrowing and controlling the work of student affairs practitioners to principally compliance functions does not connect activists and the institution to a common purpose. Student affairs practitioners have to be able to broker institutional power and mediate conflicting activists' demands. To do so, they must be empowered to engage in truly collaborative relationships with students. Only institutional leaders can make that empowerment possible.

An institution's president is the linchpin in a campus' cultural change. Though presidential power must be negotiated with boards of trustees or state governance bodies, presidents must serve as anchors to the institutional courage necessary to change the culture of gender violence and antagonism on their campuses. To do so, presidents must expose the evident and observable discursive misogyny, as well as the campus' veiled gender norms that support and foment gender violence on campus. The institutional norms and values that implicitly and explicitly reinforce gender inequity and disenfranchisement (e.g., underfunding women's centers and mental health services for survivors versus the financial privilege given men's athletics) must be challenged by the institution's executive leader. As in other institutional contexts, challenging an institution's discursive assumptions and norms is necessary to enact cultural change in the institution (Kegan and Lahey 2009). As an example, when seeking to change the culture of STEM education in universities, researchers have asserted that "problematic implicit theories" held by STEM departments and faculty can frustrate and repress efforts to change cultural norms in academia (Kezar, Gerhke, and Elrod 2015, 500). Institutional policies and practices are directed and galvanized by its culture, cultures that can "denigrate the integrity and worth of certain groups" (Kuh and Whitt 1988, v).

If, as Kuh and Whitt (1988, v) assert, "managing meaning is an important responsibility of leaders" in higher education, then college and university presidents must challenge the "meaning" of gender violence and misogyny on their campuses. They must become the architects of new gender discourses on campus that challenge the intent and purposes of campus norms that tolerate and even encourage physical and psychological gender violence. As the architects of campus culture, these institutional leaders bear the responsibility for the safety and development of all students in all campus spaces. As the architects for gender-safe campuses, presidents must lead the design for cultural change, actively overseeing and managing the structural integrity of the project. As an exercise in institutional courage, we have argued that structural change can begin by empowering student affairs practitioners to recommit to professional ethics guided by the profession's vocational ethics. As architects of cultural change on campus, our college and university presidents can make this happen.

CAMPUS SEXUAL VIOLENCE ACTIVISM NOW

After a period of abeyance in the early 2000s, student activism around ending sexual violence has been relentless and highly visible for the last decade. As we've argued in earlier chapters, several factors contribute to this, including the growth of social media platforms as a means of communication, particularly among Millennial and Gen Z–era students, and the degree of sophistication many of today's students have regarding their rights under Title IX. Armed with the knowledge that institutions must protect them, and that the stakes are extremely high for not doing so, today's sexual violence activist uses a wide variety of strategies to accelerate the urgency of ending campus sexual violence.

All the same, they also incur challenges. Rhoads (2016) noted: "Ranging from threat of life and limb, to emotional and psychological strain, to the basic costs of neglecting one's studies as a consequence of devoting time and energy to organizing, [activists] clearly incur serious costs" (199).

The urgency of their cause was perhaps never more acutely felt than during the presidency of Donald Trump (2016–2020), when Secretary of Education Betsy DeVos was empowered to dissemble many of the Obama administration's progressive improvements to college policies and practices regarding adjudication, prevention education, and accountability. As discussed in chapter 2 DeVos's rollback of protections for survivors and refusal to honor insights from decades of activism to center trauma informed practices was stark and swift, and it awakened the full power of activist recrimination.

As this project draws to a close, we are conscious of the need to consider what's next and what may drive the future work of student activists. On March 8, 2021 (International Women's Day), President Joseph R. Biden announced he would call for a commission to review the 2019 "final rule" "with an eye toward unraveling a new system put into place by former Education Secretary Betsy DeVos" (Meckler 2021). Biden called for a review of the regulations to determine coherence with the values and priorities of his administration. In the meantime, his administration issued a memorandum noting that colleges may broaden the scope of incidents they choose to investigate (in response to DeVos's highly narrow and specific definition of what constitutes sexual harassment), that they may investigate and adjudicate incidents that happen off campus if they involve students over which the institution has substantial control, and that colleges many remove accused students or employers from campus while an investigation is underway (Brown 2021).

Each of these policy directives is in direct repudiation of DeVos, and each returns the overall tenor of permitted actions to one that more closely resembles the Obama-era regulations. The controversy around the widely differing approaches to Title IX enforcement by the Obama and Trump administrations culminated in the recent highly contested nomination of Catherine Llhamon to the Department of Education's top civil rights post. Llhamon, whose Obama-era guidelines were portrayed as hostile to accused students by DeVos, was confirmed narrowly. The 50–50 senate vote required Vice President Kamala Harris to serve as the tie-breaker (Ujifusa 2021).

As an original sponsor of the 1991 Violence Against Women Act, Biden is in a unique position to claim both expertise and authority on federal regulations to oppose sexual violence. Importantly, the announced review would take place within a larger structure of policymaking, a White House Gender Policy Council. Through the establishment of the Gender Policy Council, Biden has signaled his concern that the politics driving the Trump-era changes ignored and dismissed analyses of power and identity in sexual violence. Today's CSVAs bring a commitment to the work that reflects a deep dedication to naming and dismantling operations of power in the work, along with other power vertices (race, class, [dis]ability, nationality, and other salient categories). The presidential message is that sexual violence policy-setting devoid of the analysis of power and identity is not a viable option for policy makers, student activists, or college faculty and administrators, if the goal is to end sexual violence on our campuses.

In conclusion, as we have demonstrated throughout this book and revisited in this chapter, student activists' understanding of power, their use of voice, and their deployment of strategies to enact change are inspiring to witness and have much to teach us. CSVAs recognize that collaborative relationships with student affairs practitioners and institutional leaders in which power is also collaborative allow the development of collective imaginations and cultivate safer campuses. In the absence of a commitment to collaboration and collaborative power, CSVAs, student affairs practitioners, and campus leaders will continue missing the insights each brings to the table, potentially forfeiting a campus future that is safer and in which all students can flourish unabated. To this end, we echo the sentiments of Stokes and Miller (2019), who wisely implored educators that "there must be a deliberate and organized commitment to institutional transparency. In order to know the issues, and fix the issues, you must engage with student activists" (160).

METHODOLOGICAL APPENDIX

PARTICIPANT RECRUITMENT

Campus sexual violence activists and recent alumni (class of 2014 or later) were identified on a rolling basis beginning in January 2020. These were students who were active after the "Dear Colleague" Letter and during the #MeToo movement. CSVAs were identified if publicly named in reputable news sources such as the *New York Times*, the *Washington Post*, and the *Chronicle of Higher Education,* in searches of campus newspapers, and if named in *The Hunting Ground* (Dick and Ziering 2016). Online search engine keyword searches also identified student activists highlighted in other periodicals; these sometimes confirmed those we had previously identified. Throughout the winter 2020, key informants at US institutions were contacted for referrals, and we eventually settled on a list of publicly named CSVAs.

Participants were contacted to consent to an interview approved by the institutional review board. They then were asked to refer us to other student activists, creating a chain-referral sample of potential activist interviewees. We wanted to ensure the scope of our examination was not limited to only elite colleges and universities and self-identified white women. Therefore, we made every effort to identify racially and ethnically diverse student activists in both private and public institutions with varying student body size and campus location (e.g., urban versus rural) across the United States. One male-identified participant responded to participant solicitation but declined to be interviewed. We did not include any student activists from our own institutions.

Our method of data gathering was by interview, and our intent was to listen to and center the voices of CSVAs. We designed individual semi-structured interviews with CSVAs, informed by the vast literature on campus sexual violence and campus activism, and prior research on SVA identity (Marine and Trebiascci 2018). After institutional review board approval, 36 CSVAs were contacted and asked to consent to and participate in a 60- to 75-minute interview. Those who consented to participate understood that we would record and transcribe the interview, and participants could choose to remain anonymous in our data. None of the activists who were interviewed chose anonymity, though one participant did request a pseudonym. Some participants did request that certain information remain as background information, and this was not reported in our findings. In all, 22 SVAs from 14 different institutions participated in our study. These activists graduated from or were enrolled in academic institutions at the time of the study. Their institutions vary in type, mission, and setting. Participants provided self-identification.

Because in-person interviewing could not be conducted given COVID-19 restrictions and safety, interviews were conducted on a video communication platform (Zoom) in summer through fall 2020.

Semistructured interviews were transcribed and analyzed using Dedoose, an application used for analyzing qualitative and mixed methods research. Each transcript was coded by two researchers separately, and then compared for reliability. A third member of the

PARTICIPANT	SCHOOL	RACE	GENDER
Anja	Barnard College at Columbia University	Mixed Race, Indian and Ashkenazi Jewish	Female
Yashica	Boston University	Indian	Female
Sophia	Boston University	Asian American	Female
Maya	Georgetown University	Black	Female
Kayla	Georgetown University	Mixed Race, Black and White	Female
Danu	Harvard University	Sri Lankan/Sinhalese	Female
Nylah	Howard University	Black	Female
Eli	Middlebury College	Black	Nonbinary
Rebecca	Princeton University	White	Female
Julia	Stanford University	White	Female
Subhadra	Stanford University	Indian	Female
Kara	State University of New York at Geneseo	White	Female
Emily	State University of New York at Geneseo	White	Female
Anika	University of California, Irvine	Bangladeshi	Female
Coral	University of California, Irvine	Latina	Female
Michelle	University of California, Los Angeles	White	Female
Lynnea	University of California, Los Angeles	Indian	Female
Morgan	University of Maryland, Baltimore County	Black	Nonbinary
Alexia	University of Maryland, Baltimore County	White	Female
Nadia	University of Maryland, Baltimore County	Arab American	Female
Andrea	University of North Carolina	Latina	Female
Logan	Westminster College	White	Female

research team served to ensure inter-rater reliability. Inductive analysis identified emergent themes that were significant in the data (Patton 1990; Saldaña 2015. Thematic coding and constant comparative coding then determined analytic categories (Rallis and Rossman 2012). Codes (97) were generated from 1,051 participant utterances then compared and collapsed to create categories (Charmaz 2006). Four primary categories were identified (activist self-identification; activist motivation; activist strategies; perception of effects of activism on activists and institutions) and then thematically interpreted. Activists were emailed their transcripts for member-checking and an executive summary of the analysis for input.

Interviews with participants were designed to hear and listen to their perspectives on the what, the how, and the why of their campus sexual violence activism. We asked them to share the strategies in which they engaged. We asked to hear about their motivation for sexual violence activism and why sexual violence activism was a personal commitment. We asked these activists to share with us what they believed to be the goals of their activism and how their activism affected their sense of self, their health and mental well-being, the immediate goals for their activism, and the greater purposes of that activism. Our participants often shared views on their institution's responses to sexual violence that were framed by their own perceptions of dominant discourses that inform campus culture at their college or university. We asked these activists for their recommendations for how administrators could build stronger partnerships with student activists to enact positive change. And though not part of the initial plans, we asked these activists to comment on the effects of the COVID-19 pandemic on their activism.

BIBLIOGRAPHY

ACPA–College Student Educators International. 2019. "A Bold Vision Forward: A Framework for the Strategic Imperative for Racial Justice and Decolonization." https://myacpa.org/wp-content/uploads/2021/09/SIRJD_GuidingDoc2 .pdf.

ACPA–College Student Educators International and NASPA–Student Affairs Administrators in Higher Education. 2015. "Professional Competency Areas for Student Affairs Professionals." https://www.naspa.org/images/uploads/main /ACPA_NASPA_Professional_Competencies_FINAL.pdf.

Acker, Joan. 1990. "Hierarchies, Jobs, Bodies: A Theory of Gendered Organizations." *Gender and Society* 4 (2): 139–158. http://www.jstor.org/stable/189609.

Acker, Joan. 2004. "Inequality Regimes: Gender, Class, and Race in Organizations." *Gender and Society* 20 (4): 441–464. https://doi.org/10.1177/089124320628 9499.

Acker, Sandra, and Jo Anne Dillabough. 2007. "Women 'Learning to Labour' in the 'Male Emporium': Exploring Gendered Work in Teacher Education." *Gender and Education* 19 (3): 297–316.

Ali, Russlyn. 2011. "Dear Colleague Letter." Office of Civil Rights, Department of Education. https://www2.ed.gov/about/offices/list/ocr/letters/colleague-201104 _pg19.html.

Altbach, Philip G., and Robert Cohen. 2017. "American Student Activism: The Post-Sixties Transformation." *Journal of Higher Education* 61 (1): 32–49. https://www.jstor.org/stable/1982033.

American Civil Liberties Union (ACLU). 2020. "ACLU Comment on Department of Education's Final Title IX Rule on Sexual Harassment." https://www.aclu.org/press-releases/aclu-comment-department-educations-final-title-ix-rule-sexual-harassment.

Anderson, Michelle J. 2015. "Campus Sexual Assault Adjudication and Resistance to Reform." *The Yale Law Journal* 125 (7): 1940–2005. https://www.yalelawjournal.org/feature/campus-sexual-assault-adjudication-and-resistance-to-reform.

Anderson, Monica and Skye Toor and Kenneth Olmstead and Lee Rainie and Aaron Smith. 2018. "Activism in the Social Media Age," Pew Research Center, http://www.pewinternet.org/2018/07/11/public-attitudes-toward-political-engagementon-social-media/.

Anitha, Sundari, Susan Marine, and Ruth Lewis. 2020. "Feminist Responses to Sexual Harassment in Academia: Voice, Solidarity and Resistance through Online Activism." *Journal of Gender-Based Violence* 4 (1): 9–23. https://doi.org/10.1332/239868019X15764492460286.

Arendt, Hannah. 1998. *The Human Condition.* 2nd ed. Chicago: University of Chicago Press.

Arnold, Noelle W., Lisa Bass, and Kelsey Morris. 2020. "Race, Protest, and Campus Assault." *Campus Uprisings: How Student Activists and Collegiate Leaders Resist Racism and Create Hope:* 79.

Auxier, Brooke, and Monica Anderson. 2021. "Social Media Use in 2021." *Pew Research Center* 1: 1–4.

Baker, Katie J. M. 2017. "A College Student Accused a Powerful Man of Rape. Then She Became a Suspect." *Buzzfeed News.* https://www.buzzfeednews.com/article/katiejmbaker/how-accusing-a-powerful-man-of-rape-drove-a-college-student.

Barnett, Kathy, Rebecca Ropers-Huilman, and Laura Aaron. 2008. "A Planning-Process Perspective on Student Activists' Upward Influence Attempts to Effect Campus Change." *Southern Communication Journal* 73 (4): 332–346. https://doi.org/10.1080/10417940802418833.

Barnhardt, Cassie L. 2014. "Campus-Based Organizing: Tactical Repertoires of Contemporary Student Movements." *New Directions for Higher Education* 167: 43–58.

Bartlett, Tom. 2021. "Why Are Colleges So Cowardly? Jennifer Freyd Has a Few Ideas on How Leaders Should Respond to People's Concerns." *Chronicle of Higher Education*, July 23. https://www.chronicle.com/article/why-are-colleges-so-cowardly.

Basile, Kathleen C., and Linda E. Saltzman. 2002. *Sexual Violence Surveillance; Uniform Definitions and Recommended Data Elements.* Centers for Disease Control and Prevention, National Center for Injury Prevention and Control.

Batty, David, and Elena Cherubini. 2018. "UK Universities Accused of Failing to Tackle Sexual Misconduct." *The Guardian*, March 28. https://www.theguardian.com/world/2018/mar/28/uk-universities-accused-failing-tackle-sexual-misconduct.

Bautista, Karlos. 2020. "Transformative Justice Initiative Grows in First Year at Brown." *Brown Daily Herald*, November 12, 2020. https://www.browndailyherald .com/2020/11/12/transformative-justice-initiative-grows-first-year-brown/.

Bazelon, Emily. 2015. "Have We Learned Anything from the Columbia Rape Case?" *New York Times*, May 29, 2015. https://www.nytimes.com/2015/05/29 /magazine/have-we-learned-anything-from-the-columbia-rape-case.html.

Bedera, Nicole. 2020. "Trump's New Rule Governing College Sex Assault Is Nearly Impossible for Survivors to Use. That's the Point." *Time*, May 14, 2020. https://time.com/5836774/trump-new-title-ix-rules/.

Bellows, Kate Hidalgo. 2021. "How Social Media Is Fueling Protests against Campus Sexual Assault." *Chronicle of Higher Education*, September 21, 2021. https://www.chronicle.com/article/how-social-media-is-fueling-protests-against -campus-sexual-assault?cid=gen_sign_in.

Berzofsky, Marcus, Christopher Krebs, Lynn Langton, Michael Planty, and Hope Smiley-McDonald. 2013. "Female Victims of Sexual Violence, 1994–2010." *Bureau of Justice Statistics*.

Binkley, Collin. 2020. "New Sexual Assault Rules Bolster Rights of the Accused." *ABC7News*, New York, New York. May 6. https://abc7ny.com/education/new -campus-sexual-assault-rules-bolster-rights-of-accused/6156806/.

Blanchard, Joy, Marc Weinstein, and Frank A. Rojas. 2021. "Substance Use, Sexual Violence, and the Culture Surrounding College Sports: What Can Clery Data Tell Us?" *Journal of Issues in Intercollegiate Athletics* 14: 256-267, 256.

Bogen, Katherine W., Kaitlyn K. Bleiweiss, Nykia R. Leach, and Lindsay M. Orchowski. 2019. "#MeToo: Disclosure and Response to Sexual Victimization on Twitter." *Journal of Interpersonal Violence* 36 (17–18): 8257–8288. https://doi .org/10.1177/0886260519851211.

Bonilla, Yarimar, and Jonathan Rosa. 2015. "#Ferguson: Digital Protest, Hashtag Ethnography, and the Racial Politics of Social Media in the United States." *American Ethnologist* 42 (1): 4–17.

Bottrell, Dorothy, and Catherine Manathunga, eds. 2018. *Resisting Neoliberalism in Higher Education Volume I: Seeing through the Cracks*. New York: Springer.

Boyle, Kaitlin M., and Lisa Slattery Walker. 2016. "The Neutralization and Denial of Sexual Violence in College Party Subcultures." *Deviant Behavior* 37 (12): 1392–1410. https://doi.org/10.1080/01639625.2016.1185862.

Bradley, Stefan M. 2010. *Harlem vs. Columbia University: Black Student Power in the Late 1960s*. Champaign: University of Illinois Press.

Brady, Jacqueline. 2020. "Visions of New Student Activism." *Radical Teacher* 118: 1–6.

Brenner, Alletta. 2013. "Transforming Campus Culture to Prevent Rape: The Possibility and Promise of Restorative Justice as a Response to Campus Sexual Violence." *Harvard Journal of Law & Gender* 10: 1–27. https://harvardjlg.com/wp -content/uploads/sites/19/2013/10/Brenner-Transforming-Campus-Culture.pdf.

Broadhurst, Christopher J. 2014. "Campus Activism in the 21st Century: A Historical Framing." *New Directions for Higher Education* 167: 3-15.

Brodsky, Alexandra. 2016. "Working for Change, Learning from Work: Student Empowerment and Challenges in the Movement to End Campus Gender Violence." In *Contemporary Youth Activism: Advancing Social Justice in the United*

States, edited by Jerusha M. Conner and Sonia M. Rosen, 245–261. Santa Barbara, CA: Praeger.

Brown, Jesselyn. 2000. "The Writing on the Stall: Free Speech, Equal Rights, and Women's Graffiti." In *Just Sex; Students Rewrite the Rules on Sex, Violence, Activism and Equality*, edited by Jodi Gold and Susan Villari, 77–90. Lanham, MD: Rowman & Littlefield.

Brown, Sarah. 2017. "After Meeting with DeVos, Title IX Activists Say They Still Have Many Questions." *Chronicle of Higher Education*, July 13, 2017. https:// www.chronicle.com/article/after-meeting-with-devos-title-ix-activists-say-they -still-have-many-questions/.

Brown, Sarah. 2021. "6 Things to Know about the New Title IX Guidance." *Chronicle of Higher Education*, July 20, 2021. https://www.chronicle.com/blogs /higher-ed-under-biden-harris/six-things-to-know-about-the-new-title-ix -guidance.

Brownmiller, Susan. 1975. *Against Our Will: Men, Women, and Rape.* New York: Simon and Schuster.

Buckley, Cara. 2018. "Powerful Hollywood Women Unveil Anti-Harassment Action Plan." *New York Times*, January 1, 2018. https://www.nytimes.com/2018 /01/01/movies/times-up- hollywood-women-sexual-harassment.html.

Buirski, Nancy, dir. 2017. *The Rape of Recy Taylor*. Augusta, GA: Augusta Films.

Butler, Leah C., Teresa C. Kulig, Bonnie S. Fisher, and Pamela Wilcox. 2019. "Victimization at Schools and on College and University Campuses: Historical Developments and Applications of the Opportunity Framework." In *Handbook on Crime and Deviance*, edited by Marvin D. Krohn, Nicole Hendrix, Gina Penly Hall, and Alan J. Lizotte, 53–84. London: Springer.

Campos, Leonard P. 2012. "Cultivating Cultures of Courage with Transactional Analysis." *Transactional Analysis Journal* 42 (3): 209–219.

Cantalupo, Nancy Chi. 2012. "'Decriminalizing' Campus Institutional Responses to Peer Sexual Violence." *Journal of College and University Law*, no. 38: 483–527.

Carlin, Julia, Nick Stoico, and Tonya Alanez. 2021. "UMASS Amherst Students Hold Protests over Alleged Sexual Violence at Fraternity." *The Boston Globe*, September 20, 2021. https://www.bostonglobe.com/2021/09/20/metro/after -protest-over-alleged-sexual-violence-fraternity-umass-amherst-student-leaders -call-safe-environment/?p1=BGSearch_Overlay_Results.

Carrasco, Maria. 2021. "AAU Announces New Principles to Prevent Sexual Harassment." *Inside Higher Ed*, October 27, 2021. https://www.insidehighered .com/news/2021/10/27/aau-adopts-principles-prevent-sexual-harassment.

Cauce, Ana Mari. 2018. "Sexual Harassment in Academia Is a Problem We Can Address—Together." University of Washington President's Office. https://www .washington.edu/president/2018/06/28/nasem-sexual-harassment/.

Celis, William. 1991. "Agony on Campus: What Is Rape? A Special Report: Students Trying to Draw Line between Sex and Assault." *New York Times*, January 2, 1991. https://www.nytimes.com/1991/01/02/us/agony-campus-what -rape-special-report-students-trying-draw-line-between-sex.html.

Center for Institutional Courage. n.d. *Institutional Courage Defined.* https://www
.institutionalcourage.org/.

Chan, Sewell. 2017. "Recy Taylor, Who Fought for Justice after a 1944 Rape, Dies
at 97." *New York Times,* December 29, 2017. https://www.nytimes.com/2017
/12/29/obituaries/recy-taylor-alabama-rape-victim-dead.html.

Charmaz, Kathy. 2006. *Constructing Grounded Theory: A Practical Guide through
Qualitative Analysis.* Thousand Oaks, CA: Sage.

Chou, Sophie. 2018. "Millions Say #MeToo, But Not Everyone Is Heard Equally."
The World (PRI), January 23, 2018. https://www.pri.org/stories/2018-01-23
/millions-say-metoo-not-everyone-heard-equally.

Clark, Annie. 2018. "End Rape on Campus (EROC) and the Making of
The Hunting Ground." In *The Courage to Fight Violence Against Women,*
edited by Paula L. Ellman and Nancy Goodman, 103–105. New York:
Routledge.

Cohen, Arthur M., and Carrie B. Kisker. 2010. *The Shaping of American Higher
Education: Emergence and Growth of the Contemporary System.* 2nd ed. Sterling:
Wiley & Sons.

Collins, Barbara G., and Mary B. Whalen. 1989. "The Rape Crisis Movement:
Radical or Reformist?" *Social Work* 34 (1): 61–63.

Combahee River Collective. 2014. "A Black Feminist Statement." *Women's Studies
Quarterly,* 42 (3–4, Fall/Winter): 271–280. https://doi.org/10.1353/wsq.2014
.0052.

Conner, Jerusha O. 2020. *The New Student Activists: The Rise of Neoactivism on
College Campuses.* Baltimore: Johns Hopkins University Press.

Corprew III, Charles S., and Avery D. Mitchell. 2014. "Keeping It Frat: Exploring
the Interaction among Fraternity Membership, Disinhibition, and Hypermascu-
linity on Sexually Aggressive Attitudes in College-aged Males." *Journal of College
Student Development* 55 (6): 548–562.

Creeley, Will. 2012. "Why the Office for Civil Rights' April 'Dear Colleague
Letter' Was 2011's Biggest FIRE Fight." *Foundation for Individual Rights in
Education,* January 3. https://www.thefire.org/why-the-office-for-civil-rights
-april-dear-colleague-letter-was-2011s-biggest-fire-fight/.

Crowe, Chris. 2018. *Getting Away with Murder: The True Story of the Emmett Till
Case.* New York: Penguin.

Davids, Nuraan. 2020. "Reconceiving a World Around Our Bodies: Universities,
Gender-based Violence, and Social Justice." In *University Education, Controversy
and Democratic Citizenship,* edited by Nurran Davids and Yusef Waghid, 13–30.
New York: Palgrave Macmillan.

Davis, Ben. 2014. "Columbia Student's Striking Mattress Performance." *Artnet,*
September 4, 2014. https://news.artnet.com/opinion/columbia-students
-striking-mattress- performance-92346.

Davis, Janel. 2015. "Vice President Joe Biden Urges College Students to Change
Campus Rape Climate." *Atlanta Journal-Constitution,* November 10, 2015.
https://www.ajc.com/news/local-education/vice-president-joe-biden-urges
-students-change-campus-rape-climate/PmDUoINcG5ziefZN5209cL/.

Davis, Kelly Cue, Elizabeth C. Neilson, Rhiana Wegner, and Cinnamon L. Danube. 2018. "The Intersection of Men's Sexual Violence Perpetration and Sexual Risk Behavior: A Literature Review." *Aggression and Violent Behavior,* no. 40: 83–90.

Deal, Bonnie-Elene, Lourdes S. Martinez, Brian H. Spitzberg, and Ming-Hsiang Tsou. 2020. "'I Definitely Did Not Report It When I Was Raped . . . #WeBelieve Christine #MeToo': A Content Analysis of Disclosures of Sexual Assault on Twitter." *Social Media + Society* 6 (4): https://journals.sagepub.com/doi/pdf/10 .1177/2056305120974610.

Dick, Kirby, and Amy Ziering, dir. 2016. *The Hunting Ground: The Inside Story of Sexual Assault on American College Campuses.* Los Angeles, CA: Chain Camera Pictures.

Dos Santos Bruss, Sara Morais. 2019. "Naming and Shaming or 'Speaking Truth to Power'? On the Ambivalences of the Indian 'List of Sexual Harassers in Academia' (LoSHA)." *Ephemera: Theory & Politics in Organization,* no. 4: 721–743.

Draper, Alice. 2019. "South African Universities Are Facing a Crisis of Sexual Assault Committed by Staff." *The Tempest,* May 18, 2019. https://thetempest.co /2019/05/18/news/social-justice/women-sa-universities-sexually-exploited/.

Driessen, Molly C. 2020. "Campus Sexual Assault and Student Activism, 1970–1990." *Qualitative Social Work* 19 (4): 564–579. https://doi.org/10.1177 /1473325019828805.

Evans, Meg E., and Alex C. Lange. 2019. "Supporting Student Activists: An Appreciative Inquiry." *New Directions for Student Leadership,* no. 161: 65–77. https://doi.org/10.1002/yd.20321.

Every Voice Bill, Massachusetts Senate No. S764, 2019.

Every Voice Coalition. 2021. *Every Voice—Massachusetts.* https://www .everyvoicecoalition.org/states/massachusetts.

Fair, C. Christine. 2017. "#HimToo. A Reckoning." *Buzzfeed News,* October 25, 2017. https://www.buzzfeed.com/christinefair/himtoo-a-reckoning

Farrow, Ronan. 2017. "From Aggressive Overtures to Sexual Assault: Harvey Weinstein's Accusers Tell Their Stories." *New Yorker,* October 10, 2017. https:// www.newyorker.com/news/news-desk/from-aggressive-overtures-to-sexual-assault -harvey-weinsteins-accusers-tell-their-stories.

Farrow, Ronan. 2020. "'I Haven't Exhaled in So Long': Surviving Harvey Weinstein." *New Yorker,* February 25, 2020. https://www.newyorker.com/news /q-and-a/i-havent-exhaled-in-so-long-surviving-harvey-weinstein.

Felch, Jason, and Jason Song. 2014. "UC Berkeley Students File Federal Complaints over Sexual Assault." *Los Angeles Times,* February 26, 2014. https://www.latimes .com/local/lanow/la-me-ln-berkeley-students-complaint-20140226-story.html.

Ferriss, Suzanne, and Mallory Young. 2006. "Chicks, Girls and Choice: Redefining Feminism." *Junctures: The Journal for Thematic Dialogue,* no. 6: 87–97. https:// www.semanticscholar.org/paper/Chicks%2C-Girls-and-Choice%3A-Redefining -Feminism-Ferriss-Young/8c2b6543f3fe29ff97d86e70eb4085a321ad13da.

Finley, Laura. 2013. "Stifling Activism on Campus." *Counterpunch,* November 12, 2013. https://www.counterpunch.org/2013/11/12/stifling-activism-on-campus/.

Fitzgerald, Sara. 2020. *Conquering Heroines: How Women Fought Sex Bias at Michigan and Paved the Way for Title IX.* Ann Arbor: University of Michigan Press.

Flaherty, Colleen. 2018. "Bombshell Lawsuit against Dartmouth." *Inside Higher Ed*, November 16, 2018. https://www.insidehighered.com/news/2018/11/16/federal -complaint-against-dartmouth-says-college-repeatedly-ignored-reports-three.

Florida State University. 2016. "FSU Announces Settlement in Erica Kinsman Matter." *Florida State University News.* https://news.fsu.edu/news/university -news/2016/01/25/fsu-announces-settlement-erica-kinsman-matter/.

Freedman, Estelle B. 2013. *Redefining Rape.* Cambridge, MA: Harvard University Press.

Gaston-Gayles, Joy L., Lisa E. Wolf-Wendel, Kathryn N. Tuttle, Susan B. Twombly, and Kelly Ward. 2005. "From Disciplinarian to Change Agent: How the Civil Rights Era Changed the Roles of Student Affairs Professionals." *NASPA Journal* 42 (3): 263–282.

Germain, Lauren J. 2016. *Campus Sexual Assault: College Women Respond.* Baltimore: Johns Hopkins University Press.

Gersen, Jeannie. 2020. "How Concerning Are the Trump Administration's New Title IX Regulations?" *New Yorker*, May 16, 2020. https://www.newyorker.com/news /our-columnists/how-concerning-are-the-trump-administrations-new-title-ix -regulations.

Gibbs, Nancy. 1991. "When Is It Rape?" *Time Magazine*, June 3, 1991. http:// content.time.com/time/subscriber/article/0,33009,973077-1,00.html.

Giroux, Henry. 2002. "Neoliberalism, Corporate Culture, and the Promise of Higher Education: The University as a Democratic Public Sphere." *Harvard Educational Review* 72 (4): 425–464.

Gismondi, Adam, and Laura Osteen. 2017. "Student Activism in the Technology Age." *New Directions for Student Leadership* 153: 63–74.

Gold, Jodi. 2000. "Preface: They Never Burned Their Bras." In *Just Sex: Students Rewrite the Rules on Sex, Violence, Activism and Equality*, edited by Jodi Gold and Susan Villari, xvii–xxiv. Philadelphia: Rowman & Littlefield.

Gold, Jodi, and Susan Villari, eds. 2000. *Just Sex: Students Rewrite the Rules on Sex, Violence, Activism, and Equality.* Philadelphia: Rowman & Littlefield.

Gómez, Jennifer M. 2021. "Gender, Campus Sexual Violence, Cultural Betrayal, Institutional Betrayal, and Institutional Support in US Ethnic Minority College Students: A Descriptive Study." *Violence Against Women.* https://doi.org/10 .1177/1077801221998757.

Graham, Hugh Davis. 1998. "The Storm over Grove City College: Civil Rights Regulation, Higher Education, and the Reagan Administration." *History of Education Quarterly* 38 (2): 407–429. https://www.jstor.org/stable/369849.

Gravely, Alexis. 2021. "Thoughts from the Public on Title IX." *Inside Higher Ed*, June 8. https://www.insidehighered.com/news/2021/06/08/department -education-begins-title-ix-public-hearings.

Graves, Fatima. 2020. "NWLC Responds to Department of Education's Gutting of Protections for Sexual Assault Survivors." *National Women's Law Center*, May 6. https://nwlc.org/press-releases/nwlc-responds-to-department-of -educations-gutting-of-protections-for-sexual-assault-survivors/.

Green, Erica L. 2020. "DeVos's Rules Bolster Rights of Students Accused of Sexual Misconduct." *New York Times,* May 6. https://www.nytimes.com/2020/05/06/us /politics/campus-sexual-misconduct-betsy-devos.html.

Greensite, Gillian. 2003. "History of the Rape Crisis Movement." In *Support for Survivors: Training for Sexual Assault Counselors* [CALCASA]. https://www.valor .us/2009/11/01/history-of-the-rape-crisis-movement/.

Grinberg, Emanuella. 2014. "Ending Rape on Campus: Activism Takes Several Forms." *CNN,* February 12. https://www.cnn.com/2014/02/09/living/campus -sexual-violence-students-schools/index.html.

Gross, Alan M., Andrea Winslett, Miguel Roberts, and Carol L. Gohm. 2006. "An Examination of Sexual Violence against College Women." *Violence Against Women* 12 (3): 288–300.

Grundy, Saida. 2021. "Lifting the Veil on Campus Sexual Assault: Morehouse College, Hegemonic Masculinity, and Revealing Racialized Rape Culture through the Du Boisian Lens." *Social Problems* 68 (2): 226–249.

Gumport, Patricia J. 2000. "Academic Restructuring: Organizational Change and Institutional Imperatives." *Higher Education* 39 (1): 67–91.

Gupta, Gaya, and Will Kubzansky. 2021. "Students, Alums File Federal Class Action Lawsuit against Brown Claiming U. Fails to Protect Students from Sexual Violence." *Brown Daily Herald,* August 9. https://www.browndailyherald .com/2021/08/09/students-file-federal-class-action-lawsuit-brown-sexual -violence/.

Harrington, Carol. 2021. "What Is 'Toxic Masculinity' and Why Does It Matter?" *Men and Masculinities* 24 (2): 345–352.

Harrington, Cleo M. 2017. "Take Back the Night." *The Harvard Crimson,* May 5. https://www.thecrimson.com/article/2017/5/5/take-back-the-night/.

Harris, Jessica C. 2020. "Women of Color Undergraduate Students' Experiences with Campus Sexual Assault: An Intersectional Analysis." *Review of Higher Education* 44 (1): 1–30. https://doi.org/10.1353/rhe.2020.0033.

Harris, Jessica C., and Chris Linder, eds. 2017. *Intersections of Identity and Sexual Violence on Campus: Centering Minoritized Students' Experiences.* Sterling, VA: Stylus Publishing.

Harris, Kate Lockwood. 2017. "Re-situating Organizational Knowledge: Violence, Intersectionality and the Privilege of Partial Perspective." *Human Relations* 70 (3): 263–285.

Harris, Kate Lockwood. 2019. *Beyond the Rapist: Title IX and Sexual Violence on US Campuses.* Oxford: Oxford University Press.

Harrison, Laura M., and Peter C. Mather. 2017. "Making Meaning of Student Activism: Student Activist and Administrator Perspectives." *Mid-Western Educational Researcher* 29 (2): 117–135. https://www.mwera.org/MWER /volumes/v29/issue2/V29n2-Harrison-FEATURE-ARTICLE.pdf.

Hartocollis, Anemona. 2019. "Dartmouth Reaches $14 Million Settlement in Sexual Abuse Lawsuit." *New York Times,* August 6, 2019. https://www.nytimes .com/2019/08/06/us/dartmouth-sexual-abuse-settlement.html.

Hartocollis, Anemona, and Giulia Heyward. 2021. "After Rape Accusations, Fraternities Face Protests and Growing Anger." *New York Times,* October 1.

https://www.nytimes.com/2021/10/01/education/fraternities-rape-sexual-assault
.html.

Heineman, Zachary R. 2000. "Rape Reporting Remains a Delicate Balance." *The
Harvard Crimson*, September 15. https://www.thecrimson.com/article/2000/9
/15/rape-reporting-remains-a-delicate-balancing/?page=1.

Heldman, Caroline, Alissa R. Ackerman, and Ian Breckenridge-Jackson. 2018. *The
New Campus Anti-Rape Movement: Internet Activism and Social Justice*. New
York: Lexington Books.

Heller, Jenny E. 1999. "The Coalition Calls." *The Harvard Crimson*, April 5, 1999.
https://www.thecrimson.com/article/1999/4/5/the-coalition-calls-pin-the-past/.

Hidalgo Bellows, Kate, Sarah Brown, and Megan Zahneis. 2021. "Why Nebraska
Students Won't Stop Protesting." *Chronicle of Higher Education*, August 27.
https://www.chronicle.com/article/why-nebraska-students-wont-stop-protesting.

Hill, Rob Loren, and Sapna Naik. 2021. "How Neoliberal Response to Sexual
Violence Fails: The Case of Michigan State University." *Journal of Women and
Gender in Higher Education* 14 (3): 265–282.

Hobson, Janell, and Donna E. Young. 2021. "Black Women, Sexual Violence, and
Resistance in the United States." *The Routledge Companion to Black Women's
Cultural Histories*, edited by Janell Hobson. London: Routledge.

Hong, Luoluo. 2017. "Digging Up the Roots, Rustling the Leaves: A Critical
Consideration of the Root Causes of Sexual Violence and Why Higher
Education Needs More Courage." In *Intersections of Identity and Sexual Violence
on Campus: Centering Minoritized Students' Experiences*, edited by Jessica C.
Harris and Chris Linder, 23–41. Sterling, VA: Stylus.

Hong, Luoluo, and Susan B. Marine. 2018. "Sexual Violence through a Social
Justice Paradigm: Framing and Applications." *New Directions for Student
Services*, no. 161: 21–33.

hooks, bell. 2014. *Feminism Is for Everybody: Passionate Politics*. London: Routledge.

Howell, Elizabeth F., and Sheldon Itzkowitz. 2016. "The Everywhereness of
Trauma and the Dissociative Structuring of the Mind." In *The Dissociative Mind
in Psychoanalysis: Understanding and Working with Trauma*, edited by Elizabeth F.
Howell and Sheldon Itzkowitz, 33–43. London: Routledge.

Huffman, Charlotte and Mark Smith. 2018. "UNT Student on Alleged Gang
Rape: 'I Was Just Some Piece of Meat.'" https://www.wfaa.com/article/news/local
/investigates/unt-student-on-alleged-gang-rape-i-was-just-some-piece-of-meat/287
-614961998.

Hurtado, Sarah S. 2021. "Faculty Experiences Partnering with Student Affairs
Practitioners to Address Campus Sexual Violence." *Journal of Student Affairs
Research and Practice*, 1–13. https://doi.org/10.1080/19496591.2021.1902819.

Institute for Women's Policy Research. 2018. "Violence Against Black Women—Many
Types, Far-reaching Effects." https://iwpr.org/iwpr-issues/race-ethnicity-gender
-and-economy/violence-against-black-women-many-types-far-reaching-effects/.

It's On Us. *#ItsOnUs Campaign Homepage*. Accessed May 25, 2020. https://www
.itsonus.org/.

Jaisinghani, Priyanka. 2020. "3 Ways COVID-19 Has Changed Youth Activism." *The World Economic Forum COVID Action Platform*, October 12.

https://www.weforum.org/agenda/2020/10/3-ways-covid-19-has-changed -youth-activism/.

Janosik, Steven M., and Dennis E. Gregory. 2003. "The Clery Act and Its Influence on Campus Law Enforcement Practices." *Journal of Student Affairs Research and Practice* 41 (1): 182–199.

Jaschik, Scott. 2021. "'A Predatory Culture' at U of San Francisco." *Inside Higher Ed,* October 4. https://www.insidehighered.com/quicktakes/2021/10/04 /predatory-culture-u-san-francisco.

Jesse, David. 2019. "Courts Ruling on Side of Students Accused of Sexual Assault. Here's Why." *Detroit Free Press,* March 15. https://www.freep.com/story/news /education/2019/03/15/campus-sexual-assault-cases/3160325002/https://www .freep.com/story/news/education/2019/03/15/campus-sexual-assault-cases /3160325002/.

Jessup-Anger, Jody, Elise Lopez, and Mary P. Koss. 2018. "History of Sexual Violence in Higher Education." *New Directions for Student Services,* no. 161: 9–19. https://doi-org.proxy.bc.edu/10.1002/ss.20249.

Johnston, Angus. 2011. "Chivalry and Rape on the American Campus of the 1950s." *Campus Activism* (blog), April 14. https://studentactivism.net/2011/04 /14/chivalry-and-rape-on-the-american-campus-of-the-1950s/.

Joyce, Kathryn. 2017. "The Takedown of Title IX." *New York Times,* December 5. https://www.nytimes.com/2017/12/05/magazine/the-takedown-of-title-ix.html.

Kadvany, Elena. 2018. "Office for Civil Rights Finds Title IX Violations at Stanford." *Palo Alto Online,* May 1. https://www.paloaltoonline.com/news/2018 /05/01/Office-for-civil-rights-finds-title-ix-violations-at-stanford.

Kantor, Jody, and Megan Twohey. 2017. "Harvey Weinstein Paid Off Sexual Harassment Accusers for Decades." *New York Times,* October 5. https://www .nytimes.com/2017/10/05/us/harvey-weinstein-harassment-allegations.html.

Katz, Jennifer, and Melinda DuBois. 2013. "The Sexual Assault Teach in Program: Building Constructive Campus-Wide Discussions to Inspire Change." *Journal of College Student Development* 54 (6): 654–557.

Keating, AnaLouise. 2012. *Transformation Now! Toward a Post-oppositional Politics of Change.* Champaign: University of Illinois Press.

Keene, Louis. 2021. "YU Student Accuses Basketball Player of Rape, Says School Fell Short." *Forward,* August 26. https://forward.com/fast-forward/474711/yu -student-accuses-basketball-player-of-rape-says-school-investigation/.

Kegan, Robert, and Lisa Laskow Lahey. 2009. *Immunity to Change: How to Overcome It and Unlock Potential in Yourself and Your Organization.* Cambridge, MA: Harvard Business Press.

Kenneally, Meghan. 2019. "Michigan State Student Alleges Traumatic Gang Rape by Basketball Players and the School's Reaction." *ABCNews.* https://abcnews.go.com /US/michigan-state-student-alleges-traumatic-gang-rape-basketball/story?id =62331180.

Kerner, Laura Lynn, Jim Kerner, and Susan D. Herring. 2017. "Sexual Assaults on College Campuses." *Journal of Academic Administration in Higher Education* 13 (2): 41–47.

Kettrey, Heather Hensman, and Robert A. Marx. 2019. "The Effects of Bystander Programs on the Prevention of Sexual Assault across the College Years: A Systematic Review and Meta-Analysis." *Journal of Youth and Adolescence* 48 (2): 212–227.

Kezar, Adrianna. 2010. "Faculty and Staff Partnering with Student Activists: Unexplored Terrains of Interaction and Development." *Journal of College Student Development* 51 (5): 451–480.

Kezar, Adrianna, Sean Gehrke, and Susan Elrod. 2015. "Implicit Theories of Change as a Barrier to Change on College Campuses: An Examination of STEM Reform." *Review of Higher Education* 38 (4): 479–506.

Kingkade, Tyler. 2013. "Sexual Assaults Mishandled at Dartmouth. Swarthmore, USC Complaints Say." *Huffington Post,* May 24. https://www.huffpost.com /entry/sexual-assaults-mishandled-dartmouth-swarthmore_n_3321939.

Kingkade, Tyler. 2014. "The Woman behind #SurvivorPrivilege Was Kicked Out of School after Being Raped." *Huffington Post,* June 12. https://www.huffpost .com/entry/survivor-privilege-wagatwe-wanjuki_n_5489170.

Kingkade, Tyler. 2018. "Betsy DeVos Wants New Regulations That Protect Students Accused of Sexual Assault and Their Schools." *Buzzfeed News,* November 18. https://www.buzzfeednews.com/article/tylerkingkade/betsy -devos-title-ix-sexual-assault-protects-accused.

Kirkpatrick, Clifford, and Eugene Kanin. 1957. "Male Sex Aggression on a University Campus." *American Sociological Review* 22 (1): 52–58.

Klein, Renate. 2018. "Sexual Violence on US College Campuses: History and Challenges." In *Gender Based Violence in University Communities: Policy, Prevention and Educational Initiatives,* edited by Sundari Anitha and Ruth Lewis, 63–82. Cambridge: Policy Press.

Koestner, Katie. 2000. "The Perfect Rape Victim." In *Just Sex: Students Rewrite the Rules on Sex, Violence, Equality, and Activism,* edited by Jodi Gold and Susan Villari, 30–39. New York: Rowman & Littlefield.

Koller, Alex M. 2020. "Student Activists Demand Harvard Enact Amnesty Policy for Reporters of Sexual Violence." *The Harvard Crimson,* November 12. https://www.thecrimson.com/article/2020/11/12/ohcdb-amnesty-coronavirus.

Koss, Mary P., Christine A. Gidycz, and Nadine Wisniewski. 2018. "The Scope of Rape: Incidence and Prevalence of Sexual Aggression and Victimization in a National Sample of Higher Education Students." *Journal of Consulting and Clinical Psychology* 55 (2): 162–170.

Koss, Mary, and Alexandra Rutherford. 2018. "What We Knew About Date Rape Then, and What We Know Now." *The Atlantic,* September 26. https://www .theatlantic.com/ideas/archive/2018/09/what-surveys-dating-back-decades -reveal-about-date-rape/571330/.

Kowalik, Eric A. 2011. "Engaging Alumni and Prospective Students through Social Media." In *Higher Education Administration with Social Media,* edited by Laura A. Wankel and Charles Wankel. Bingley, UK: Emerald Group Publishing Limited.

Krantz, Laura, and Julia Carlin. 2021. "It's Baffling That They Exist: Some Students Call on UMASS to Rein in Fraternities." *The Boston Globe,* November 27.

https://www.bostonglobe.com/2021/11/27/metro/its-baffling-that-they-exist
-some-students-call-umass-rein-fraternities-sharing-disturbing-experiences.

Krebs, Christopher, Christine Lindquist, Marcus Berzofsky, Bonnie Shook-Sa,
Kimberly Peterson, Michael Planty, and J. Stroop. 2016. *Campus Climate Survey
Validation Study: Final Technical Report*. Washington, DC: BJS, Office of Justice
Programs.

Kreibaughm, Andrew. 2019. "College Groups Blast DeVos Title IX Proposal."
Inside Higher Ed, January 31. https://www.insidehighered.com/news/2019/01
/31/higher-ed-groups-call-major-changes-devos-title-ix-rule.

Kuh, George D., and Elizabeth J. Whitt. 1988. *The Invisible Tapestry. Culture in
American Colleges and Universities*. ASHE-ERIC Higher Education, Report
No. 1, 1988. Washington, DC: Association for the Study of Higher Education.

Kuhn, Thomas. 2021. *The Structure of Scientific Revolutions*. 3rd ed. Princeton, NJ:
Princeton University Press.

Lacey, Linda J. 1994. "We Have Nothing to Fear But Gender Stereotypes: Of
Katie and Amy and Babe Feminism." *Cornell Law Review* 80 (3): 612–645.

Laoire, Ní, Caitríona, Carol Linehan, Uduak Archibong, Ilenia Picardi, and Maria
Udén. 2021. "Context Matters: Problematizing the Policy/Practice Interface in
the Enactment of Gender Equality Action Plans in Universities." *Gender, Work &
Organization* 28 (2): 575–593.

Lester, Jaime, and Margaret W. Sallee. 2017. "Troubling Gender Norms and the
Ideal Worker in Academic Life." In *Critical Approaches to Women and Gender in
Higher Education*, edited by Pamela L. Eddy, Kelly Ward, and Tehmina Khwaja,
115–138. New York: Palgrave Macmillan.

Lewis, Ruth, and Susan Marine. 2015. "Weaving a Tapestry, Compassionately:
Toward an Understanding of Young Women's Feminisms." *Feminist Formations*:
118-140.

Lewis, Ruth, and Susan B. Marine. 2018. "Student Feminist Activism to Challenge Gender Based Activism." In *Gender Based Violence in University Communities: Policy, Prevention, and Educational Initiatives*, edited by Anitha Sundari and
Ruth Lewis, 129–147. Cambridge: Policy Press.

Lewis, Ruth, and Susan B. Marine. 2020. "Reflecting On and Looking Forward to
Transformation." In *Collaborating for Change: Transforming Cultures to End
Gender-Based Violence in Higher Education*, edited by Susan B. Marine and Ruth
Lewis. Oxford: Oxford University.

Lewis, Ruth, Susan Marine, and Kathryn Kenney. 2018. "'I Get Together with My
Friends and Try to Change It': Young Feminist Students Resist 'Laddism,' 'Rape
Culture' and 'Everyday Sexism.'" *Journal of Gender Studies* 27 (1): 56–72.
https://doi.org/10.1080/09589236.2016.1175925.

Lhamon, Catherine E., and Vanita Gupta. 2016. "Dear Colleague Letter on Transgender Students." *U.S. Department of Education*, May 13. https://www2.ed.gov/about
/offices/list/ocr/letters/colleague-201605-title-ix-transgender.pdf.

Li, Manyu, Nadia Turki, Cassandra R. Izaguirre, Chloe DeMahy, Brooklyn
Laberty Thibodeaux, and Taylor Gage. 2021. "Twitter as a Tool for Social
Movement: An Analysis of Feminist Activism on Social Media Communities."
Journal of Community Psychology 49 (3): 854–868.

Linder, Chris. 2018. *Sexual Violence on Campus: Power-Conscious Approaches to Awareness, Prevention, and Response*. Bingley, UK: Emerald Group Publishing.

Linder, Chris, Jess S. Myers, Colleen Riggle, and Marvette Lacy. 2016. "From Margins to Mainstream: Social Media as a Tool for Campus Sexual Violence Activism." *Journal of Diversity in Higher Education* 9 (3): 231.

Linder, Chris, and Jessica S. Myers. 2017. "Intersectionality, Power, Privilege, and Campus-Based Sexual Violence Activism." In *Intersections of Identity and Sexual Violence on Campus: Centering Minoritized Students' Experiences*, edited by Chris Linder and Jessica Harris, 175–193. Sterling, VA: Stylus Publishing.

Linder, Chris, Stephen John Quaye, Alex C. Lange, Meg E. Evans, and Terah J. Stewart. 2019a. *Identity-Based Student Activism: Power and Oppression on College Campuses*. New York: Routledge.

Linder, Chris., Stephen J. Quaye, Alex C. Lange, Rickey E. Roberts, Marvette C. Lacy, and Wilson Kwamogi Okello. 2019b. "'A Student Should Have the Privilege of Just Being a Student': Student Activism as Labor." *Review of Higher Education* 42 (5): 37–62.

Linder, Chris, Stephen J. Quaye, Terah J. Stewart, Wilson K. Okello, and Ricky Erika Roberts. 2019c. "'The Whole Weight of the World on My Shoulders': Power, Identity, and Student Activism." *Journal of College Student Development* 60 (5): 527–542.

Lindgren, Simon. 2019. "Movement Mobilization in the Age of Hashtag Activism: Examining the Challenge of Noise, Hate, and Disengagement in the #MeToo Campaign." *Policy & Internet* 11 (4): 418-438.

Lipsett v. University of Puerto Rico, 864 F.2d 881 (1st Cir. 1988).

Locke, Benjamin D., and James R. Mahalik. 2005. "Examining Masculinity Norms, Problem Drinking, and Athletic Involvement as Predictors of Sexual Aggression in College Men." *Journal of Counseling Psychology* 52 (3): 279.

Lonsway, Kimberly A., and Louise F. Fitzgerald. 1994. "Rape Myths. In Review." *Psychology of Women Quarterly* 18 (2): 133–164.

MacGregor, Wendy. 2018. "It's Just a Game Until Someone Is Sexually Assaulted: Sport Culture and the Perpetuation of Sexual Violence by Athletes." *Education & Law Journal* 28 (1): 43–73.

MacKinnon, Catharine A. 1979. *Sexual Harassment of Working Women: A Case of Sex Discrimination*. New Haven, CT: Yale University Press.

MacKinnon, Catharine A. 1989. *Toward a Feminist Theory of the State*. Cambridge, MA: Harvard University Press.

Manning, Kathleen, Jillian Kinzie, and John Schuh. 2012. *One Size Does Not Fit All: Traditional and Innovative Models of Student Affairs Practice*. New York: Routledge.

Marine, Susan. 2018. "Sexual Violence on College Campuses." In *Contemporary Issues in Higher Education,* edited by Marybeth Gasman and Andrés Castro Samayoa. New York: Routledge.

Marine, Susan B. 2011. *Stonewall's Legacy: Bisexual, Gay, Lesbian, and Transgender Students in Higher Education: AEHE*. Vol. 152. Hoboken, NJ: John Wiley & Sons.

Marine, Susan B., and Sarah Hurtado. 2020. "Association for the Study of Higher Education (ASHE) Response to The Department of Education's May 2020 regulations on Title IX of the Higher Education Act of 1972 (Nondiscrimination on the Basis of Sex in Education Programs or Activities Receiving Federal Financial Assistance)." *Association for the Study of Higher Education.* Accessed September 14, 2021. https://www.ashe.ws/Files/Position%20Taking/2021.03%20ASHE%20 Response%20to%20ED's%20May%202020%20regulations%20on%20Title%20 IX%20of%20the%20Higher%20Education%20Act%20of%201972.pdf.

Marine, Susan, and Ruth Lewis. 2019. "Mutuality without Alliance: The Roles of Community in Becoming a College Student Feminist." *Gender and Education* 31 (7): 886–902.

Marine, Susan B., and Ruth Lewis, eds. 2020. *Collaborating for Change: Transforming Cultures to End Gender-Based Violence in Higher Education.* Oxford: Oxford University Press.

Marine, Susan B., and Z Nicolazzo. 2017. "The Rise of Compliance Culture: A Dead End for Ending Campus Sexual Violence." *Praxis: The Blog of the Journal of Critical Scholarship in Higher Education and Student Affairs.* https://jcshesa .wordpress.com/2017/06/27/the-rise-of-compliance-culture-a-dead-end-for -ending-campus-sexual-violence.

Marine, Susan B., and Z Nicolazzo. 2020. "Campus Sexual Violence Prevention Educators' Use of Gender in Their Work: A Critical Exploration." *Journal of Interpersonal Violence* 35 (21–22): 5005–5027. https://doi.org/10.1177 /0886260517718543.

Marine, Susan, and Ashley Trebisacci. 2018. "Constructing Identity: Campus Sexual Violence Activists' Perspectives on Race, Gender, and Social Justice." *Journal of College Student Development* 59 (6): 649–665.

Markowitt, Xenia. 2009. "Is It My Job to Teach the Revolution?" *Chronicle of Higher Education,* October 11. https://www.chronicle.com/article/is-it-my-job -to-teach-the-revolution/.

Martínez Alemán, Ana M. 2000. "Race Talks: Undergraduate Women of Color and Female Friendships." *Review of Higher Education* 23 (2): 133–152.

Martínez Alemán, Ana M. 2014. "Managerialism as the 'New' Discursive Masculinity in the University." *Feminist Formations* 26 (2): 116.

Martínez-Alemán, Ana M., and Katherine Lynk Wartman. 2008. *Online Social Networking on Campus: Understanding What Matters in Student Culture.* New York: Routledge.

McCabe, Caitlin, and Andy Thomason. 2013. "Complaint: UNC Pressured Dean to Underreport Sexual Assault Cases." *Daily Tarheel,* January 17. https://www .dailytarheel.com/article/2013/01/50f8ca9bc71da.

McCaffrey, Kait. 2019. "Laser Focus without Limits: UMBC Grads Choose Their Own Adventures." *University of Maryland Baltimore County News,* May 16. https://umbc.edu/stories/laser-focus-without-limits-umbcs-newest-grads-choose -their-own-adventures.

McCart, Wes R. 2008. "Simpson v. University of Colorado: Title IX Crashes the Party in College Athletic Recruiting." *DePaul Law Review* 58: 153–184.

McFadden, Robert D. 2005. "Remembering Columbia, 1968." *New York Times Archive.* https://archive.nytimes.com/cityroom.blogs.nytimes.com/2008/04/25 /remembering-columbia-1968.

McGuire, Danielle L. 2004. "'It Was Like All of Us Had Been Raped': Sexual Violence, Community Mobilization, and the African American Freedom Struggle." *Journal of American History* 91 (3): 906–931.

McGuire, Danielle. 2010. *At the Dark End of the Street: Black Women, Rape, and Resistance—A New History of the Civil Rights Movement from Rosa Parks to the Rise of Black Power.* New York: Vintage.

McKinley, James G. 2018. "3 Women Accuse Weinstein of Sexual Assault in Federal Suit." *New York Times*, June 1. https://www.nytimes.com/2018/06/01 /nyregion/harvey-weinstein-class-action-suit.html.

McMahon, Sarah, and G. Lawrence Farmer. 2011. "An Updated Measure for Assessing Subtle Rape Myths." *Social Work Research* 35 (2): 71–81.

McMahon, Sarah, Judy L. Postmus, Corianne Warrener, and Ruth Anne Koenick. 2014. "Utilizing Peer Education Theater for the Primary Prevention of Sexual Violence on College Campuses." *Journal of College Student Development* 55 (1): 78–85.

McMahon, Sarah, Leila Wood, and Julia Cusano, and Lisa M. Macri. 2019. "Campus Sexual Assault: Future Directions for Research." *Sexual Abuse* 31 (3): 270–295.

Meckler, Laura. 2021. "Biden Directs Fresh Review of Title IX Rule on Campus Sexual Assault." *Washington Post*, March 8, 2021. https://www.washingtonpost .com/podcasts/daily-202-big-idea/biden-directs-fresh-review-of-title-ix-rule-on -campus-sexual-assault/.

Mehren, Elizabeth. 2002. "Harvard Is Sued for Its New Sex Assault Policy." *Women's ENews*, December 8, 2002. https://www.feminist.com/news/news130.html.

Melnick, Merrill. 1992. "Male Athletes and Sexual Assault." *Journal of Physical Education, Recreation & Dance* 63: 32–35.

Melnick, R. Shep. 2018. *The Transformation of Title IX: Regulating Gender Equality in Education.* Washington DC: The Brookings Institution.

Mendes, Kaitlynn, Jessica Ringrose, and Jessalynn Keller. 2018. "#MeToo and the Promise and Pitfalls of Challenging Rape Culture through Digital Feminist Activism." *European Journal of Women's Studies* 25 (2): 236–246.

Mendes, Kaitlynn, Jessica Ringrose, and Jessalyn Keller. 2019. *Digital Feminist Activism: Girls and Women Fight Back Against Rape Culture.* Oxford: Oxford University Press.

Méndez, Xhercis. 2020. "Beyond Nassar: A Transformative Justice and Decolonial Feminist Approach to Campus Sexual Assault." *Frontiers: A Journal of Women Studies* 41 (2): 82–104.

Meyerson, Debra E., and Maureen A. Scully. 1995. "Crossroads Tempered Radicalism and the Politics of Ambivalence and Change." *Organization Science* 6 (5): 585–600.

Milano, Alyssa. 2017. "If You've Been Sexually Harassed or Assaulted Write 'me too' as a Reply to This Tweet." Twitter, October 15. https://twitter.com/Alyssa _Milano/status/919659438700670976.

Miller, Chanel. 2019. *Know My Name.* New York: Viking.

Miller, Michael T., and David V. Tolliver III, eds. 2017. *Student Activism as a Vehicle for Change on College Campuses: Emerging Research and Opportunities.* Hershey, PA: IGI Global.

Mitra, Shayoni. 2015. "'It Takes Six People to Make a Mattress Feel Light . . .': Materializing Pain in Carry That Weight and Sexual Assault Activism." *Contemporary Theatre Review* 25 (3): 386–400.

Monroe, Stephanie. 2006. "Dear Colleague Letter." Office of Civil Rights, Department of Education, January 25. https://www2.ed.gov/about/offices/list/ocr/letters/sexhar-2006.html.

Moore, Sarah. 2011. "Tracing the Life of a Crime Category: The Shifting Meaning of 'Date Rape.'" *Feminist Media Studies* 11 (4): 451–465.

Mordecai, Lorin. 2017. "Sexual Violence in Intercollegiate Athletics: A Historical Perspective of Male Athletic Entitlement." *Journal of Issues in Intercollegiate Athletics*, special issue: 36-56.

Morgan, Demetri, and Charles Davis. 2019. *Student Activism, Politics, and Campus Climate in Higher Education.* New York: Routledge.

Morris, Edward W., and Kathleen Ratajczak. 2019. "Critical Masculinity Studies and Research on Violence against Women: An Assessment of Past Scholarship and Future Directions." *Violence Against Women* 25 (16): 1980–2006.

Moylan, Carrie A., and McKenzie Javorka. 2020. "Widening the Lens: An Ecological Review of Campus Sexual Assault." *Trauma, Violence, & Abuse* 21 (1): 179-192.

Mumby, Dennis K., and Cynthia Stohl. 1991. "Power and Discourse in Organization Studies: Absence and the Dialectic of Control." *Discourse & Society* 2 (3): 313–332.

Murnen, Sarah K., and Maria H. Kohlman. 2007. "Athletic Participation, Fraternity Membership, and Sexual Aggression among College Men: A Meta-Analytic Review." *Sex Roles* 57 (1–2): 145–157.

Murphy, Amy, and Brian Van Brunt. 2016. *Uprooting Sexual Violence in Higher Education: A Guide for Practitioners and Faculty.* London: Routledge.

New, Jake. 2015. "Justice Delayed." *Inside Higher Ed.* May 6, 2015. https://www.insidehighered.com/news/2015/05/06/ocr-letter-says-completed-title-ix-investigations-2014-lasted-more-4-years.

New York State Education Law, Article 129-B, Senate Bill No. S5965, 2015.

Odell, Jenny. 2020. *How to do nothing: Resisting the attention economy.* Brooklyn, NY: Melville House.

O'Donnell, Jessica. 2022. "Feminist Retaliation in the Digital Age." In *Gamergate and Anti-Feminism in the Digital Age*, pp. 139-177. Tyne and Wear, UK: Palgrave.

Oliver, Kelly. 2016. *Hunting Girls: Sexual Violence from the Hunger Games to Campus Rape.* New York: Columbia University Press.

O'Neill, Cathy. 2022. *The Shame Machine: Who Profits in the New Age of Humiliation.* New York: Crown.

Paglia, Camille. 1992. *Sex, Art and American Culture: Essays.* New York: Vintage.

Pandit, Vivek. 2015. *We Are Generation Z: How Identity, Attitudes, and Perspectives Are Shaping Our Future.* London: BrownBooks.

Parker, John N., and Edward J. Hackett. 2012. "Hot Spots and Hot Moments in Scientific Collaborations and Social Movements." *American Sociological Review* 77 (1): 21–44.

Patterson, Jennifer. 2016. *Queering Sexual Violence: Radical Voices from within the Anti-Violence Movement.* New York: Riverdale Avenue Books.

Patton, Michael Quinn. 1990. *Qualitative Evaluation and Research Methods.* Beverly Hills, CA: Sage.

Pauly, Madison. 2020. "Betsy DeVos Rewrote Campus Sexual Assault Rules, But Survivor Activists Aren't Backing Down." *Mother Jones,* August 27. https://www .motherjones.com/politics/2020/08/devos-campus-sexual-assault-title-ix/

Pellegrini, Ann. 2018. "#MeToo: Before and After." *Studies in Gender and Sexuality* 19 (4): 262–264.

Pérez-Peña, R. 2014. "Students File Complaints on Sexual Assaults at Columbia University." *New York Times.* April 25. https://www.nytimes.com/2014/04/25 /nyregion/accusations-over-assault-at-columbia.html

Pérez-Peña, R. 2014b. "Rare Survey Examines Sexual Assault at M.I.T." *New York Times.* October 28. https://www.nytimes.com/2014/10/28/us/rare-survey -examines-sex-assault-at-mit-.html

Peruta, A., and Christina Helm. 2018. "University Facebook Pages: Engaging the Alumni Community in the Digital Era." *Journal of Social Media in Society* 7 (1): 123–150.

Pettit, Emma. 2020. "The Next Wave of #MeToo." *Chronicle of Higher Education,* February 16. https://www.chronicle.com/article/The-Next-Wave-of-MeToo /248033.

Phipps, Alison. 2018. "'Lad Culture' and Sexual Violence Against Students." In *Routledge Handbook of Gender and Violence,* edited by Nancy Lombard, 171–182. New York: Routledge.

Piller, Ingrid, and Jinhyun Cho. 2013. "Neoliberalism as Language Policy." *Language in Society,* no. 42: 23–42.

Potter, Sharyn, Rebecca Howard, Sharon Murphy, and Mary M. Moynihan. 2018. "Long-term Impacts of College Sexual Assaults on Women Survivors' Educational and Career Attainments." *Journal of American College Health* 66 (6): 496–507.

Prior, Sarah, and Brooke de Heer. 2021. "Everyday Terrorism: Campus Sexual Violence and the Neoliberal University." *Sociology Compass* 15 (9): e12915.

Pryal, Katie Rose Guest. 2018. "Held Accountable: An Interview with Andrea Pino." *Women in Higher Education,* August 1. https://www.wihe.com/article -details/78/held-accountable-an-interview-with-andrea-pino/.

Rallis, Sharon F., and Gretchen B. Rossman. 2012. *The Research Journey: Introduction to Inquiry.* New York: Guilford Press.

Reis, Elizabeth. 2012. *American Sexual Histories,* vol. 1. New York: John Wiley & Sons.

Rentschler, Carrie A. 2018. "#MeToo and Student Activism against Sexual Violence." *Communication Culture & Critique* 11 (3): 503–507.

Reynolds, Celene. 2019. "The Mobilization of Title IX across US Colleges and Universities, 1994–2014." *Social Problems* 66 (2): 245–273.

Rhoads, Robert A. 2016. "Student Activism, Diversity, and the Struggle for a Just Society." *Journal of Diversity in Higher Education* 9 (3): 189–202.

Ringel, Cheryl. 1997. *Criminal Victimization in 1996, Changes 1995–1996 with Trends 1993–1996.* Washington, DC: Bureau of Justice Statistics, US Department of Justice.

Rogers, Katie, and Erica L. Green. 2021. "Biden Will Revisit Trump Rules on Campus Sexual Assault." *New York Times,* March 8. https://www.nytimes.com /2021/03/08/us/politics/joe-biden-title-ix.html.

Roiphe, Katie. 1993. *The Morning After: Sex, Fear, and Feminism on Campus.* Chicago: Little, Brown.

Ropers-Huilman, Becky, Laura Carwile, and Kathy Barnett. 2005. "Student Activists' Characterizations of Administrators in Higher Education: Perceptions of Power in 'the System.'" *Review of Higher Education* 28 (3): 295–312.

Rose, Vicki M. 1977. "Rape as a Social Problem: A Byproduct of the Feminist Movement." *Social Problems* 25 (1): 75–89.

Rossi, Andrew, dir. 2014. *Ivory Tower.* Atlanta, GA: CNN Films.

Rowan-Kenyon, Heather T., and Ana M. Martínez Alemán. 2016. *Social Media in Higher Education: ASHE Higher Education Report* 42 (5). John Wiley & Sons.

Saldaña, Johnny. 2015. *The Coding Manual for Qualitative Researchers.* Thousand Oaks, CA: Sage.

Salter, Michael. 2013. "Justice and Revenge in Online Counter-Publics: Emerging Responses to Sexual Violence in the Age of Social Media." *Crime, Media, Culture* 9 (3): 225–242.

Sanday, Peggy Reeves.1996. "Rape-prone versus Rape-free Campus Cultures." *Violence Against Women* 2 (2): 191–208.

Sandler, Bernice R. 1981. "Sexual Harassment: A Hidden Problem." *Educational Record* 62 (1): 52–57.

Schein, Edgar H. 1991. "What Is Culture." In *Sociology of Organizations: Structures and Relationships,* edited by Mary Ellen Godwyn and Jody Hoffer Gittell, 243–253. Newbury Park, CA: Sage.

Schwartz, Karen. 1990. "College Students Scrawl Names of Alleged Rapists on Bathroom Walls." *AP News,* November 28. https://apnews.com/857412cf1b739 af2e0f536fbe6a64327.

Scott, Ellen K. 2000. "Everyone against Racism: Agency and the Production of Meaning in the Anti-Racism Practices of Two Feminist Organizations." *Theory and Society* 29 (6): 785–818. https://www.jstor.org/stable/3108529.

Seabrook, Rita C., Sarah McMahon, and Julia O'Connor. 2018. "A Longitudinal Study of Interest and Membership in a Fraternity, Rape Myth Acceptance, and Proclivity to Perpetrate Sexual Assault." *Journal of American College Health* 66 (6): 510–518.

Seabrook, Rita C., L. Monique Ward, and Soraya Giaccardi. 2018. "Why Is Fraternity Membership Associated with Sexual Assault? Exploring the Roles of Conformity to Masculine Norms, Pressure to Uphold Masculinity, and Objectification of Women." *Psychology of Men and Masculinity* 19 (1): 3.

Sheidlower, Jesse. 2009. *The F-Word.* Oxford: Oxford University.

Silbaugh, Katharine. 2015. "Reactive to Proactive: Title IX's Unrealized Capacity to Prevent Campus Sexual Assault." *Boston University Law Review* 95: 1049–1073.

Sinko, Laura, Michelle Munro-Kramer, Terri Conley, T., and Denise Saint Arnault. 2021. "Internalized Messages: The Role of Sexual Violence Normalization on

Meaning-Making after Campus Sexual Violence." *Journal of Aggression, Maltreatment & Trauma* 30 (5): 565–585.

Smith, Carly Parnitzke, and Jennifer J. Freyd. 2013. "Dangerous Safe Havens: Institutional Betrayal Exacerbates Sexual Trauma." *Journal of Traumatic Stress* 26 (1): 119–124.

Soave, Robby. 2015. "How *The Hunting Ground* Spreads Myths about Campus Rape." *Reason*, November 11. https://reason.com/2015/11/20/how-the-hunting -ground-spreads-lies-abou/#.

Staros, Karolina. 2018. "Campus Sexual Assault: Addressing Rape Culture and Creating Lasting Change." In *Rape Cultures and Survivors: An International Perspective*, edited by Tuba Inal and Merrill D. Smith, 85-100. 2 vols. Santa Barbara, CA: Praeger.

Steinberg, Terry Nicole. 1991. "Rape on College Campuses: Reform through Title IX." *Journal of College and University Law* 18: 39–72.

Stokes, Sy, and Donte' Miller. 2019. "Remembering 'The Black Bruins': A Case Study of Supporting Student Activists at UCLA." In *Student Activism, Politics, and Campus Climate in Higher Education*, edited by Demetri L. Morgan and Charles H. F. Davis III, 143–163. New York: Routledge.

Strauss, Valerie. 2020. "Betsy DeVos's Controversial New Rule on Campus Sexual Assault Goes into Effect." *Washington Post*, August 14. https://www .washingtonpost.com/education/2020/08/14/betsy-devoss-controversial-new -rule-campus-sexual-assault-goes-into-effect/.

Sullivan, Oriel, Jonathan Gershuny, and John P. Robinson. 2018. "Stalled or Uneven Gender Revolution? A Long-Term Processual Framework for Understanding Why Change Is Slow." *Journal of Family Theory & Review* 10 (1): 263–279.

Take Back the Night Foundation. 2021. "History of Take Back the Night." https://takebackthenight.org/history/.

Tani, Karen M. 2016. "An Administrative Right to Be Free from Sexual Violence: Title IX Enforcement in Historical and Institutional Perspective." *Duke Law Journal* 66: 1847–2017.

Taylor, Kate. 2015. "Mattress Protest at Columbia University Continues into Graduation Event." *New York Times,* May 19, 2015. https://www.nytimes.com /2015/05/20/.

Thelin, John. 2018. *Going to College in the Sixties.* Baltimore: Johns Hopkins University Press.

Tracy, Marc. 2015. "Jameis Winston Files Countersuit against Accuser." *New York Times*, May 9. https://www.nytimes.com/2015/05/10/sports/football/ jameis -winston-files-counterclaims-against-accuser.html.

Tuerkheimer, Deborah. 2021."To Address Sex Assault on College Campuses, End the Culture of Victim Blaming.*" Chicago Tribune*, October 3. https://www .chicagotribune.com/opinion/commentary/ct-opinion-sexual-assault-college -campuses-victim-blaming-20211001-evqf42pcangeznpxdfkdmo3a5a-story.html.

Ujifusa, Andrew. 2021. "Senate Confirms Catherine Lhamon to Civil Rights Post; Kamala Harris Casts Decisive Vote." *EdWeek*, October 20. https://www.edweek .org/policy-politics/senate-confirms-catherine-lhamon-to-civil-rights-post -kamala-harris-casts-decisive-vote/2021/10.

United States Congress. 1992. *S.1150—Higher Education Amendments of 1992.* https://www.congress.gov/bill/102nd-congress/senate-bill/1150.

United States Department of Education. 2014. "U.S. Department of Education Releases List of Higher Education Institutions with Open Title IX Sexual Violence Investigations." *United States Department of Education.* https://www.ed.gov/news/press-releases/us-department-education-releases-list-higher-education-institutions-open-title-ix-sexual-violence-investigations.

United States Department of Education. 2017. "Department of Education Issues New Interim Guidance on Campus Sexual Misconduct." *United States Department of Education,* September 22. https://www.ed.gov/news/press-releases/department-education-issues-new-interim-guidance-campus-sexual-misconduct.

United States Department of Education Office for Civil Rights. 1997. "Sexual Harassment Guidance: Harassment of Students by School Employees, Other Students, or Third Parties." United States Department of Education Office for Civil Rights. https://www2.ed.gov/about/offices/list/ocr/docs/sexhar01.html.

United States Department of Education Office for Civil Rights. 2008. "Sexual Harassment: It's Not Academic." United States Department of Education Office for Civil Rights. https://www2.ed.gov/about/offices/list/ocr/docs/ocrshpam.pdf.

United States Department of Education Office for Civil Rights. 2018. *Nondiscrimination on the Basis of Sex in Education Programs or Activities Receiving Federal Financial Assistance: Notice of Proposed Rulemaking.* Washington, DC: Federal Register Archives. https://www.federalregister.gov/documents/2018/11/29/2018-25314/nondiscrimination-on-the-basis-of-sex-in-education-programs-or-activities-receiving-federal.

United States District Court, District of Massachusetts. 2016. "*John Doe V. Brandeis*: Memorandum and Order on Defendant's Motion to Dismiss." United States District Court, District of Massachusetts. https://www.govinfo.gov/content/pkg/USCOURTS-mad-1_15-cv-11557/pdf/USCOURTS-mad-1_15-cv-11557-0.pdf.

van der Kolk, Bessel. 2014. *The Body Keeps the Score: Brain, Mind, and Body in the Healing of Trauma.* New York: Penguin.

Volokh, Eugene. 2016. "Lawsuit Alleging Columbia's Sex Assault Investigation Was Biased against Him Because He Was Male." *Washington Post,* July 29. https://www.washingtonpost.com/news/volokh-conspiracy/wp/2016/07/29/student-may-go-forward-with-lawsuit-alleging-columbias-sex-assault-investigation-was-biased-against-him-because-he-was-male/.

Walker, Edward T., Andrew W. Martin, and John D. McCarthy. 2008. "Confronting the State, the Corporation, and the Academy: The Influence of Institutional Targets on Social Movement Repertoires." *American Journal of Sociology* 114 (1): 35–76.

Walker, Grayson Sang. 2010. "Evolution and Limits of Title IX Doctrine on Peer Sexual Assault." *Harvard Civil Rights - Civil Liberties Law Review,* no. 45: 95–133.

Walker, James. 2020. "Betsy DeVos Sued by Organizations Representing Student Victims of Sexual Violence." *Newsweek,* June 11. https://www.newsweek.com/betsy-devos-lawsuit-title-ix-rule-changes-sexual-harassment-1510147.

Walsh, Molly. 2018. "#HerToo: Middlebury Student in Trouble over List of Accused Sexual Transgressors." *Seven Days.* January 24. https://www.sevendaysvt

.com/vermont/hertoo-student-in-trouble-over-list-of-accused-sexual
-transgressors/Content?oid=12090461.

Wanjuki, Wagatwe. 2017. "Foreword." In *Intersections of Identity and Sexual Violence on Campus: Centering Minoritized Students' Experiences,* edited by Jessica C. Harris and Chris Linder, i–xvii. Sterling, VA: Stylus.

Wantland, Ross A. 2008. "Our Brotherhood and Your Sister: Building Anti-rape Community in the Fraternity." *Journal of Prevention & Intervention in the Community* 36 (1–2): 57-73.

Warner, Tara D., Christopher T. Allen, Bonnie S. Fisher, Christopher P. Krebs, Sandra Martin, and Christine H. Lindquist. 2018. "Individual, Behavioral, and Situational Correlates of the Drugging Victimization Experiences of College Women." *Criminal Justice Review* 43 (1): 23-44.

Warshaw, Robin. 1988. *I Never Called It Rape: The Ms. Report on Recognizing, Fighting and Surviving Date and Acquaintance Rape.* New York: Sarah Lazin Books.

Wegner, Rhiana, Antonia Abbey, Jennifer Pierce, Sheri E. Pegram, and Jacqueline Woerner. 2015. "Sexual Assault Perpetrators' Justifications for Their Actions: Relationships to Rape Supportive Attitudes, Incident Characteristics, and Future Perpetration." *Violence Against Women* 21 (8): 1018–1037.

West, Carolyn M. 1995. "Mammy, Sapphire, and Jezebel: Historical Images of Black Women and Their Implications for Psychotherapy." *Psychotherapy: Theory, Research, Practice, Training* 32 (3): 458–466.

White, Aaronette M. 2001. "I Am Because We Are: Combined Race and Gender Political Consciousness among African American Women and Men Anti-Rape Activists." *Women's Studies International Forum* 24 (1): 11–24.

Whitehead, Alfred North. 1967. *The Aims of Education and Other Essays.* New York: Free Press.

Wiersma-Mosley, Jacquelyn D., and Kristen N. Jozkowski. 2019. "A Brief Report of Sexual Violence among Universities with NCAA Division I Athletic Programs." *Behavioral Sciences* 9 (2): 17.

Williams, Lee Burdette. 2015. "The Dean of Sexual Assault." *Inside Higher Ed,* August 7. https://www.insidehighered.com/views/2015/08/07/how-sexual
-assault-campaign-drove-one-student-affairs-administrator-her-job-essay.

Wolf-Wendel, Lisa E., Susan B. Twombly, Kathryn Nemeth Tuttle, Kelly Ward, and Joy L. Gaston-Gayles. 2004. *Reflecting Back, Looking Forward: Civil Rights and Student Affairs.* Washington, DC: NASPA.

Wooten, Sara Carrigan, and Roland W. Mitchell, eds. 2015. *The Crisis of Campus Sexual Violence: Critical Perspectives on Prevention and Response.* London: Routledge.

Yung, Corey Rayburn. 2015. "Is Relying on Title IX a Mistake." *University of Kansas Law Review,* no. 64: 891–914.

Zahneis, Megan, and Vimal Patel. 2020. "Covid-19 Changes the Calculus of Grad Student Activism." *Chronicle of Higher Education,* April 30. https://www.chronicle
.com/article/covid-19-changes-the-calculus-of-grad-student-activism/.

Zounlome, Nelson OO, Y. Joel Wong, Elyssa M. Klann, Jessica L. David, and Nat J. Stephens. 2019. "'No One . . . Saves Black Girls': Black University Women's Understanding of Sexual Violence." *The Counseling Psychologist* 47 (6): 873–908.

INDEX

accountability, for sexual violence, 124; institutional, 39–44, 45, 79, 139–40, 163–66; of sexual violence perpetrators, 22, 23, 42, 49–50, 75, 112–13, 141, 160–63, 169, 182–83; social justice paradigm, 164–66

adjudication procedures, 79; due process, 20, 44, 45; evidential requirements, 40–41, 42, 118; grievance processes, 30–31; mismanagement, 37, 50–54, 55, 68; restorative and transformative justice approach, 161–63; revisions, 2–3, 37, 161, 182–83; transparency, 64

administrators. *See* leadership, institutional

Alabama Committee for Equal Justice for Mrs. Recy Taylor, 23–24

alcohol consumption, role in sexual violence, 73–74, 75, 76, 96, 163–64, 175, 179

Allred, Gloria, 47, 51

alumni, 6, 51–52, 54, 60–61, 83, 100, 142–43

American Civil Liberties Union, 3

American College Personnel Association-College Student Educators International, 155–56

American College Personnel Association / National Association of Student Personnel Administrators (ACPA/ NASPA), 155–56

Anika, 10–11, 66, 69, 104, 116

Arendt, Hannah, 136–37

Arizona State University, 89

Arpino, Emily, 12, 70, 74–75, 113–14, 115, 119